Management Guru Lord Krishna

O.P. Jha

DIAMOND BOOKS

Publisher : **Diamond Pocket Books (P) Ltd.**
X-30, Okhla Industrial Area, Phase-II
New Delhi-110020
Phone : 011-40712100, 41611861
Fax : 011-41611866
E-mail : wecare@diamondbooks.in
Website : www.diamondbooks.in
Edition : 2025
Printed by : Repro (India)

Management Guru Lord Krishna
By - O.P. Jha

Foreword

In the last quarter of the twentieth century, Management emerged as an important discipline. In the first decade of the twenty first century it became the most popular subject. Besides technocrats, medicos, planners, bureaucrats and economists, commoners have also taken interest in this discipline.

In this domain, we find some definitive books by expert and for experts; and some topic specific books too. There is a flood of general books that claim affiliations with the discipline of management. Sometimes they're pleasing and sometimes they're confusing.

Lord Krishna is the most popular personality in India. After a span of thousands of years he still stimulates the imagination of poets and the common man find an ever increasing interest in him. We find varieties to the maximum extent in his life. This was not possible without the management of highest order, whether this management might be on the level of the creator of this universe or at the level of human being of extraordinary capacity. In India, most of the people regard and respect Lord Krishna as the perfect incarnation of God, the almighty. Yet others regard him the most developed soul. Some people regard him as an extraordinary human being. Opinions may differ but all regard him something extraordinary. Hence, curiosity in his life knows no limit.

People from management field or from any other walk of life need a glimpse of Lord Krishna's life. Going through some portions of his life draws certain aspects of management skill, though not in pure definitive terms. This book is an endeavor to put a light on some of those aspects of Lord Krishna's life which may ignite a spark in the mind of ordinary individual and provide a solace to wavering souls. No doubt, there're some useful stuffs in this book for the specialists too. This book will help people to understand the cause of conflicts at international level. And this will inspire them to seek solutions to the conflicts.

The author of the book could find this endeavor into a concrete shape under the able leadership of the publisher of Diamond Books, Mr. N.K.Verma who is an extra ordinary bibliophile. He loves to represent the ancient wisdom of mankind in a sophisticated format through book and enjoys travelling always through unexplored territories too. Hence, he publishes an amazing range of books and journals. Great! …….. Great indeed!

My heart expresses gratitude to all who directly or indirectly helped me to bring this book into a shape and to get access to its lovers, the readers. No doubt, my family members, wife Mamata Jha and son Abhinav Chaitanya have helped me to complete this task with full dedication.

Yours ever

O.P. Jha

E-mail: opjha189@gmail.com

Contents

Part IV Management Guru Lord Krishna and Solution for International Conflict

Part I
Limitless Horizons

1. Krishna as a Guru

कृष्णाम् नारायाणम् वन्दे कृष्णाम् जगद्गुरुम्।
कृष्णाम् द्वौपायनम् वन्दे कृष्णाम् पृथा सुतम्॥

– श्रीमद्भागवत

Krishnam Narayanam Vande Krishnam Jagadgurum Krishnam Dwaupayam Vande Krsihnam Pritha sutam

– *From* **'Shrimadbhagavata'**

Meaning: *We salute Krishna as the supreme soul, Narayana and as the Guru of this world. With him we also salute Dwapayan , the author of The Bhagavata and Arjuna, the son of Pritha (Kunti).*

When one goes through the available literatures on the life of Lord Krishna, one enters a realm of wonder. Is it possible to have so many varieties and attributes in the life of a single person? On the basis of the presence of extraordinary attributes and variety in his life, people worship him as the supreme God.

As a child he was affectionate to all in his neighbourhood. As a boy he was the centre of attraction among girls. As a warrior he was respected by the mighty warriors of his time. He was dutiful son, a faithful friend, a dedicated husband (despite having many wives), a successful diplomat, a skillful strategist, a visionary planner, a flag bearer of righteousness, and a best model for all time.

All his attributes left an indelible mark on the mile stones of time and spirit. But a guru he left an inspiring permanent footprint. We see him as a guru in all walks of life. Let me clarify the term guru first. A guru is just not a master or spiritual master. **A guru is one who relieves his disciple from all kinds of bondage and makes his life blissful**. A guru is above all trifles.

When he was a toddler of mere a week, a wicked ogress (Pootna) came to kill him. She was in a lady's guise. She had applied a deadly poison on his breasts. She tried to feed Krishna. The boy had a developed sense of test. He could discriminate between his mother's breasts and that of enemy's. Thinkers attach many philosophical connotations to this episode but for the purpose of this book it is plain to conclude that he couldn't be befooled by disguise. **A genuine guru doesn't come under the influence of false impression and inspires his followers to understand the truth and recognise facts.**

Krishna never ignores life. He seeks the beauty of life equally amidst chaos and harmony. Spiritual is never indifferent to material. Negation of life in the name of spiritual is like ignoring food but talking wellness.

He enjoys the company of friends but his friends had no doubt that he is above them. He is the leader among them. A leader enjoys his team but his teammates recognise his capabilities. In games, Krishna's childhood friends used to enjoy equal status but whenever there was any problem they called their saviour, Krishna. **A guru may look one among equals but he is always fulfilled with the spirit to excel.**

All milkmaid girls of Braja had love for Krishna. He had also the same feeling. His love wasn't specific. But there was a special place for Radha in his heart. He didn't pronounce his special inclination for Radha even once. But his associates were trained enough to understand his for and against. When ever Radha enjoyed the company of Krishna, other girls didn't disturb them. **A guru without any pronouncement makes his intention clear. His followers execute His mission.**

Krishna as a guru is seen best in his form just before the war of Mahabharata. It was clear that a war on major scale is going to be fought in the battlefield of Kurukshetra. Armies of Pandavas and Kaurvas assembled there. Before the actual battle Arjuna, mighty warrior among Pandavas came along with Krishna between the both armies. Arjuna was enveloped in a sentimental thought. He wasn't ready to kill his kith and kin. He was ready to surrender.

This is a common weakness. Usually people are overpowered by such thoughts. There is always a bottleneck to achieve a mission/goal/target. Sometimes one's attitude, sometimes family relations, sometimes political disturbances, friendship or other such things come in the way. **A genuine guru dispels such darkness and put a beam of light before his disciple, so that the disciple couldn't relinquish his duty.**

People become sentimental and relinquish their duty. A guru makes them aware of the importance of duty and put a clear concept of duty before them.

For Arjuna, the war of Mahabharata was to be fought for the sake of throne. But for Krishna, this was not a battle for succession. He was to uproot the very cause of war. People fight battle but overlook the cause and genesis of war. After Mahabharata no major war was fought in India. No world war was fought here. Only battles were fought.

For Arjuna, Duryodhana was his opponent. For Krishna, Duryodhana was a symbol of wicked force. He was to eliminate the cause of all evils. He was to establish the realm of righteousness.

Krishna took Arjuna into confidence and preached him to observe his duty. He put his philosophy forcefully and logically to convince Arjuna. His sermons become popular and the entire body of his preaching in the battle field is known as the Gita. Literary it is a collection of songs. Here sermons become songs to be sung by all. This book isn't related to any sect. It's a universal song. In fact, it's a manifesto of understanding life.

We can't make one believe at once. It takes time to make one understand. In the first chapter of the Gita, Arjuna pronounces his weakness and dejected mood. In the second chapter, Krishna preaches the knowledge of immortality of soul. But for a dejected person, immortality of soul doesn't make a point. After this, Lord Krishna focuses his intention on the theory of righteousness. But even this doesn't convince him. Arjuna is convinced only when Krishna shows his Super human attributes. Before this, Arjuna was respecting him as his friend and guide but after the tenth and eleventh chapters the tones of both Krishna and Arjuna changed. Here Krishna emerges as a guru and Arjuna is overwhelmed with pleasure to be his disciple.

When one recognises the capacity of his guru, one is convinced. Arjuna accepted Krishna as his guru. After the acceptance, Krishna preaches the importance of duty, devotion and knowledge. Arjuna understands that Duryodhana is the representative of evil forces. To establish peace and make the world prosper, it is necessary to eliminate Duryodhana.

After this understanding, Arjuna fought the war. To perform duty skillfully one needs an intellectual bent of mind that is never influenced by sentiments. To be emotional is good, to be kind is better and to be poetic is the best. But the best poetry comes out of the depth of the truth. The Gita is full of such depths. It has become an essential compendium for all those who aspire to prosper and flourish in life. The Gita is a beautiful flower sprang out of Krishna's extraordinary life and immortal life philosophy. Management guru Lord Krishna is a reflection of Guru Lord Krishna, the eternal. We'll find glimpses this guru in the succeeding chapters.

Here, I salute the universal guru Lord Krishna (Vande Krishnam Jagadgurum)!

2. Gunas of Lord Krishna and Management

गुणात्मनस्तेऽपि गुणान् विमांतु
हितावतीर्णस्य क ईशिरेऽस्य।
कालेन यैर्वा विमिताः सुकल्पै-
र्भूपांशवः खे मिहिकाद्युभासः॥

- श्रीमद्भागवत

Gunatamanste api Gunan Vimatu
Hitavateernashya Ka Eeshireashya
Kalen Yairva vimitah sukalpair
Mupanshavah khe Mihikadyu bhashah

– *From* ***'Shrimadbhagavata'***

Meaning: *Who is able to determine the attributes of Lord Krishna who takes birth for the welfare of this world? He is the shelter of all positive attributes. One can count all the dust particles of this earth and all the stars of the galaxy but one can't count His attributes.*

But for the pleasure of readers sixty four attributes of Lord Krishna have been mentioned here on the basis of

- 'Baktirasamrit Sindhu'

(Written by Roop Goswami.)

In the tenth chapter of **the Gita**, Lord Krishna proclaims that wherever there is a good thing i.e. a beautiful thing, it is the reflection of God, the almighty. In fact, there is glory of God in all things divine. Ultimately Krishna says that he himself dwells in all these beautiful things. He admits that he lives in living as well as non-living things. According to **The Bhagvata Mahapurana,** no one can mention the glory of God. His attributes (qualities) are beyond description. But poets try to describe these attributes for the sake of ultimate pleasure or what we call bliss. According to the same sacred book, in the beginning of the world God created sixteen attributes. These were made by sixteen faculties of the God almighty. There are five sense organs in our body, there are five work organs in our body, and there are five elements (Earth i.e. solid element, water, fire, air and ether) and psyche. All these sixteen faculties constitute human body. All the sixteen faculties are never in perfect position in human beings. They are up to a proportion in a normal human being. Related to these faculties, there're sixteen attributes.

We find the mention of creation of this world in the Bhagvata. In this vast treasure of devotion, there's a description of God's creation and acceptance of these sixteen attributes to run this world. In human beings we find some of these attributes. In India, Krishna is regarded as the perfect incarnation of God. Some people mention his sixteen arts (solah kalayen) and some others mention his sixty four attributes (chausadh gunas) and still some others remain satisfied by the six characteristics (lakshana) of God only. Let us see, what are these attributes, arts and characteristics. In sixty four attributes, we find the inclusion of sixteen arts and six characteristics.

Rupa Goswami was a famous poet-saint in the group of Chaitanya Mahprabhu. He had mentioned sixty four attributes of Lord Krishna in his famous book "**Bhaktirasamrit Sindhu**"(The Ocean of devotional nectar). I would like to describe these qualities in brief. Some of these qualities are found in all human beings but all of these can't be found in a single human being. In Lord Krishna all these qualities were present. These are:

Beautiful Body Organs (Suramyangah)

Lord Krishna's body organs were in perfect shape. They were beautiful. Physical beauty has no match. It attracts attention of people. A smart person, a beautiful person has many fans. Physical constitution is the first point in an individual's persona. Other qualities are counted only after appearance. One can have well chiseled body through proper exercise, yoga and meditation. But a beautiful body is a gift from God. Lord Krishna was called Shyamsunder (sunder means beautiful/handsome). He was a prince charming for the girls of his neighbourhood. Even during his youth, women and girls were always keen to win Krishna's favour. A beautiful body has always a plus point.

Confluence of All Beautiful Attributes (Sarvalakshan Samanvitah)

Krishna's personality was a confluence all beautiful and auspicious qualities. Auspicious qualities give pleasure to one and all. It is said that flowers bloomed, trees bore fruits and sages sang the hymns form the Vedas at the time of his birth. Kings invited him in their royal ceremonies. Mothers invited him at dinner. Girls invited him in gardens for rendezvous. His presence was always regarded as auspicious.

Pleasure-giving (Ruchirah)

Krishna's glittering personality was giving pleasure tot the viewers. It was soothing to eyes. He gave blissful pleasure to his foster mother Yashoda through his childhood divine acts. He gave pleasure to his childhood friends, milkmaid boys of Braja through games and plays. He gave pleasure to the young girls of Braja by his dance, drama, song and sweet talks. He gave pleasure to noble persons by ending the terror of demons and wicked persons. Those who take care of others give pleasure to many. His personality becomes pleasing one. Lord Krishna had a pleasing personality since his birth. All adored, loved and worshipped him.

Full of Light (Tejsauktah)

His personality was full of light. It was radiating lights as the Sun radiates continuously. When he gave Arjuna divine eyes to take a glance of His cosmic form, he saw the Lord having the light of thousands of moons, suns and stars. A radiant personality sparkling light and dignity is adored by all. Many persons weren't able to look at his face continuously. They had to be aside.

Mighty (Baliyan)

He was full of strength. He was very mighty. He killed many wicked demons that were creating terror in this world. Sometimes, to tackle wicked one has to prove that might is right, though this isn't an ideal situation. Non - violence had no meaning for the demons sent by Kansa to kill Krishna. Krishna passed his childhood in Braja (a region in the District Mathura, India). People of Braja innocent and righteous. But Kansa's soldiers continued to harass them. Annihilation of the wicked was possible only through might. Sometimes to save the innocent, to establish an order and to maintain the rule of the law, elimination of the evil is must. Here, the might counts. Might must be employed for a good cause.

Tenderness/Adolescence (Vayasanvitah)

Krishna was always looking like an adolescent. His personality was full of delicacy and tenderness. Looking younger is the dream of everyone. People do a lot of things to remain younger. Some people go to gyms. Others take help of some chemical or Ayurvedic medicine to keep oneself fit and younger. There's a story of sage Chavan who in the evening of his life decided to attain his youth again. He discovered a medicine to remain young for ever. This is an eternal quest for mankind to remain young. Those who look younger win friends and influence people.

Knowledge of Many Languages (Vividhavahuvidbhashavida):

Krishna had knowledge of many languages. On the basis of his multilingual capacity, he could interact freely with the kings and diplomat of many countries and regions. In today's multilingual world mono-linguistic is insufficient. One should be at least diglot. Either to sale one's product or to interact with people one needs the knowledge of target group. Those who don't know the language of his target group have to take help of interpreters and translators. Sometimes these professions distort the soul of the text. In the present context, English is an international language. Mandarin (a major Linguistic group in China) has a large following segment in China's population. More than 800 million people speak Hindi. But for advertisement only local language is a desirable tool. Buddha chose local language Pali instead of Sanskrit, the language of scholars to spread his message. One should know lingua franca as well as a local language. Tulsidas decided to compose his great epic the Ramcharitmanas in Avadhi, a local language.

Great linguists of modern time are of the opinion that polyglots have developed mind power. They can think on many dimensions. Their mind becomes more resourceful and creative. Lord Krishna was the creative of highest order. He had knowledge of many languages.

Truthful (Satyavakyah)

Krishna was always truthful. He didn't tell lies. People easily believe a truthful person. A truthful person commands the respect of his colleagues and masses. This is an essential attribute for leadership. Even during the Mahabharata war he didn't tell a lie. Even Udhishthira, the righteous eldest Pandava had to tell a pseudo truth. But Lord Krishna himself didn't tell a lie. During his childhood he was hiding something from his foster Mother Yashoda but his gesture happened to be so innocent that it used to pronounce the truth. It was enough for Yashoda to understand the truth. Truth is the first pillar of righteousness.

Sweet Spoken (priyamvada)

Merely speaking truth isn't sufficient. One shouldn't speak bitter truth. One should have mellifluous tongue. Lord Krishna used to speak mellifluously even with dreaded criminals. He never loosed his temper. Speaking a sweet language is only possible when one has a balanced personality. Lord Krishna conveys even a strong message through sweet words. Talking tough in sweet words needs a higher level of balanced personality. Even in a war like situation, diplomats talk sweetly. We can get much through sweet language.

Speaking an ear soothing language isn't a childish endeavor. It demands a much organised inner engineering—engineering of mind/psyche. It is quite different from "a honey tongue and a heart of gale." If there's a bottleneck somewhere in your mind, you can't speak a sweet language for a longer period. You can't suppress your intention for a longer period, particularly through artificial effort. Lord Krishna was speaking sweetly with sweet girls of Braja and he continued to do so even during the war of Mahabharata. His sermon just before the devastating war is known as the Gita (A divine song). It's the epitome of Krishna's greatness that a warrior sings a divine song even in the battlefield.

Expert in Rhetoric (Vavdukah)

Lord Krishna was expert in the art of delivering speeches. This art is known as Rhetoric. This art needs knowledge of many disciplines. The speaker should have the knowledge of particular time and occasion and he must know the person or the audience with whom he interacts. Krishna was the master in this art. This is difficult art. Everyone can't be a good orator. Oratory is in important point of management skill. A good orator wins favour of many persons. Through his oratory he eliminates hurdles from his path. This needs much expertise. A good orator turns the audience in his favour. One should understand the nerve of the occasion for an effective speech.

Krishna was acting like a kid before his mother/parents. He was behaving like a handsome and smart youth in the company of his friends. He was talking the language of a strategist in the battlefield. He was using the language of the diplomat in the company of kings. He was above mundane affairs in the eyes of his devotees. This is art. This is rhetoric.

A Scholar in Many Branches of Studies (Supandityah)

Krishna was an omniscient incarnation. He had knowledge of all braches of knowledge. He started his formal studies in at the age of 12. After killing the wicked king of Mathura, Kansa, he was sent to the gurukula (a school in ancient India). From human point of view, before this stage, he had seen the life from a close point. He had acquired both sweet and bitter experiences. He had to remain twelve years away from his parents. They were imprisoned by Kansa. Though his foster mother Yashoda dedicated her complete life for the boy Krishna, he was aware of the fact. He enjoyed the company of dedicated friends and beautiful girls. He had killed a dozen of dreaded demons. All these experiences made him mature enough (from God's point of view, he had all the skills by birth) But human beings learn through different stages in the life. In his gurukula of sage Sandipini, he learnt all the sixty four attributes, sixteen arts and fourteen branches of study prevalent in ancient India only in a brief period of sixty four days.

In today's knowledge society one should be a widely read man to handle the situation tactfully and to deliver expected result. A variety of exposure needed in this multi - tasking age.

Intelligent (Buddhiman)

If one is beautiful but not intelligent, one won't be able to get a proper place in life. Only an intelligent person can excel in life. Lord Krishna was very sharp since his childhood. Today people talk about emotional intelligence. If the intelligence is employed to have a relationship at emotional level, it's ethical but in the most of the cases emotions are employed to emotionally blackmail people. In the world of ads, people earn dividend on the basis of harnessing people's emotion. But ultimate thing is the quality of a product. If the quality has a standard, it survives. Fake coins have no worth. Krishna always used his emotional as well as intelligence for the pleasure of the people having righteous heart. Emotional intelligence is ephemeral. I would like to use **righteous intelligence** instead of emotional intelligence. Let me clarify the term righteous intelligence. A righteous intelligence is guided by one's conscience. It's never employed for vested interest and befooling others. It doesn't play with others emotions. It gives benefit to one and all. It's a long term strategy. It's core of sustainable development. In the future corporate sector and big giants will survive only on the basis of righteous intelligence. It's not sectarian. It's not subjective. Despite being a matter of heart, it has rational connotations. One conscience can separate grains from the chaffs. Here, there's no conflict between what is secular and what is righteous. Righteousness can be employed in the both spiritual and secular contexts. This kind of intelligence is productive in real sense i.e. production with sustainability. Hence the righteous intelligence. Lord Krishna employed this kind of intelligence.

In most of the cases, business house become bankrupt, people faces the onslaught of economic retardation due to lack of righteous intelligence. If there's righteous intelligence, there will be no corruption. **There must be a test for righteous intelligence quotient in the selection process of executives and bureaucrats**. The present context doesn't permit me for further elaboration.

In the domain of righteous intelligence, we'll find co-operation in the arena of competition. Hence, a better business environment and a better world order. It can transform the work culture of the entire globe. Hence, there will a metamorphosis of corporate culture. **There'll be beauty in the work and peace in the mind.**

Genius (Pratibhasampanna)

Lord Krishna had an extraordinary genius. He understood his world very quickly. From incarnation angle, the world is the result of his grace. But on the basis of the life he had led, he was a genius. His all senses were in perfect order. We call someone genius when he/she does something beyond the capacity of an intelligent person. Genius is the higher stage of intelligence. Krishna did most of the extraordinary things in his life. When we employ a good chunk of our potential, we are intelligent. Most of the human beings don't employ even one percent of their potential in their entire life. A genius uses at least 1/6 of his potential. An intelligent person uses from 1/10 to 1/9 or 1/8 of his potential. Krishna used his potential both in love and war. He played games with his milk maid friends. He was the main strategist in the Mahabharata war. He showed his cosmic form to Arjuna. This was the greatest show of potential. No human being can do it. But a human being can use his potential to a better extent. To excel is the duty of a man. One should strive for excellence.

Expert in All Arts (Vidagdh or Kala Nipunah)

Lord Krishna had mastery in all arts. He was a good warrior, musician, singer, dancer etc. Those who are master of many arts have importance in industry. In today's multitasking age, one should be master of many arts, crafts and skills. He was at home in martial arts. He was a hero among his colleagues. Despite his busyness, he could spare a fair amount of time for his queens. He used to comb his queens sometimes. He was a source of fear for foes and a fountain of pleasure for friends. He could balance the all ends of life with a great mastery on the basis of his expertise in many arts. Flute was his main musical instrument. He was so fond of it that he couldn't spare it even for his beloved Radha. He used to keep his flute even during the war of the Mahabharata.

In ancient India, there was no sharp demarcation between various disciplines. Though there were many subjects in existence. In arts, people meant craft and science also. It was a comprehensive term used for various disciplines. Knowledge of various arts and crafts makes one a resourceful person. Such a person is in much demand. He can interact at various levels. Industry needs a multi dimensional personality. That's why there is much thrust on extra-curricular activities. Exposure to various activities enhances the capacity of human brain.

Skilful and Cautious (Chaturah)

Lord Krishna was able to solve many problems simultaneously. An individual handle one or two assignments at a time. But Krishna was handling many portfolios simultaneously. He was enjoying the company of milk maid boys but was always aware of untoward happenings. He killed many demons during his childhood, particularly during plays. Without the death of Duryodhana, there was no end of the Mahabharata war. To establish a righteous society, to lay the foundation of the rule of the law, death of Duryodhana was essential. Duryodhana's mother Gandhari had never opened a bandage on her eyes since her marriage with the blind prince Dhritarashtra. She told his eldest son, Duryodhana, to come naked before her. She would open her eyes and by the rays of her eyes his body would be strong more that stones. No weapon, even a thunder bolt would be able to break his body. Pandavas, the friends of Lord Krishna had no knowledge of such a thing. But he was so intelligent, skillful and cautious that he could know the intention of Duryodhana. When he was going naked before his mother, Lord Krishna appeared there. He told him— "O, Duryodhana, you are going to his mother. Your mother has a bandage on her eyes since her marriage. She hadn't seen you even at the time of your birth. First time she will see you, when you're a grown up. Please, put at least a leaf around your waist. You should follow ethical practice." By his intelligence he aroused Duryodhana's conscience. He put a leaf around his waist. Gandhari watched the entire body of her son. The entire body of Duryodhana became strong except his waist and thigh. During his last battle with Bhima, he couldn't bear the hit of Bhima's club on his comparatively weak parts. He met his end. To establish the rule of law, one has to be clever on some occasions.

At Home in (Dakshah)

Lord Krishna could fulfill many difficult tasks in a short span of time. Solving difficult problems in a short span of time is the demand of all time but it is important in the modern fast changing world.

People take assignments in haste for the sake of making money even though he isn't at home in fulfilling those assignments. Doing any recklessly doesn't pay any dividend. Even if it pays, it pays at the cost of one's brand. Getting anything at the cost of one's brand is nothing less than self annihilation. It's like moving towards a suicidal path. Those who're in any profession or in the pursuit of provide service is brands in themselves or in the processing of being made a brand. Therefore, **accepting the assignment which you're at home in is the mantra of the time.** Krishna was at home in whatever he did : in war and peace, in love and romance, in art and craft, in study and art, in performing his duty—as a son, as a husband, as a lover, as a father, as a friend, as a disciple, as a guru etc.

Gratefulness (Kritajna)

It is better to forget the bitter experiences of the past but one should be grateful to all helps. Lord Krishna couldn't forget his childhood friends. He couldn't forget good people. To remember anyone's help is gratefulness. The survival of human civilisation depends on gratefulness. In absence of gratefulness, we find a nude exhibition of opportunism in many spheres of life. Krishna never forgot his friend Sudama. When he came to Krishna after the gap of many years, for some help, Krishna welcomed him as the most revered guest. He paid due honour to his gurukula friend. He helped him thoroughly. He never forgot his childhood friend Radha. She was always in his heart. They met after a gap of hundred years but recognised each other. This is called love. He never forgot his foster mother Yashoda, even though he couldn't meet her often. He helped his friends Pandavas in all their needs. He was a friend in need, so he was a friend in deed. Once his forefinger was cut severely and it was bleeding profusely. There was nothing to stop bleeding. Draupadi was present there. She tore a portion of her precious sari and with that piece she bandaged his finger. Lord Krishna didn't forget this scene in his entire life. When Dushasana, the second son of Dhritarashtra tried to pull her sari and tried to made her nude in the assembly of noble persons of Hastinapur's court. Lord Krishna saved the dignity of Draupadi. This is called Gratefulness.

Friendship is a higher stage. It's not liaison work. It's beyond the precinct of P.R. work. It's difficult to find a real man. It's very difficult to find a real friend. **He who has a friend can't be a poor fellow**. By boarding the boat of a real friendship one can sail through vicious tornadoes.

Strong Determination (Sudidhvrata)

There's an old saying—"where there is a will, there is a way." On the basis of strong determination people mounted the Mount Everest. People crossed the Pacific, landed on the moon, walked on the virgin territories. Wars are won not only by strong armies and weapons, but by strong determination. Lord Krishna was a man of strong determination. Once he decided to establish the rule of righteousness, he did so at any cost. Sometimes he had to sacrifice much to fulfill this task.

A man of strong determination, never succumb to hurdles. Many lusts, attractions and deviations come in the way. Those who get lured by such things don't reach their destinations and meet their destiny. A man of strong determination can never be swayed by such lusts. Krishna never let any adjustment flourish at the cost of his mission. For a man of strong determination, his destination becomes his destiny. For the weak, destiny is destination.

There're two ways to look at the life. William Shakespeare said: "Character is destiny." But the famous novelist Thomas Hardy said—"Destiny is character." No one can differ from the fact that sometimes situations in life become so fluid that an individual is swayed by "what is going on." In their middle age most of the persons start believing in status quo. For a man of determination, even the goal isn't the end of the game. He changes his destiny to reach his destination. At last people start believing in his acts. We find an aura around him. Such a man is called man of strong determination.

Lord Krishna decided to kill Kansa. He did so. He decided to marry Rukmini. He did so. He decided to end the dark age of Kaurvas' reign. He achieved so. Besides, other factors the role of his strong determination was pivotal.

Knowledge of Time, Space and Person (Deshkalsupatrajna)

Before taking any action, Lord Krishna always took place, person and time into consideration. Before taking any decision, one should always consider, whether it is the right moment to proceed, whether it is the place for the action or whether it is the right person to deal with. Krishna left Mathura and didn't wage further war with Jarasandha. When Lord Krishna killed Kansa, the wicked king of Mathura and appointed Sursen, as the king of Mathura. Jarasandha, the father-in-law of Kansa, became furious and started harassing the innocent subjects of Mathura. Many times Lord Krishna defeated him. But Jaransandha was unwilling to stop his terror. At last he decided to leave Mathura. He made Dwarka, a famous sea port on the western coast of India his capital. He made proper arrangement of killing of Jarasandha during a sacrifice organised by Udhishthira many years after. Bhima killed Jarasandha. So the consideration of time, space and person is essential to succeed in life.

Before any major decision, any huge investment a manager takes the factor of time, space and person into consideration. These factors are influential in all walks of life. A strategist, a planner never overlooks these factors. He knew that as long as Karna had a divine weapon, divyastra, Krishna's friend Arjuna was not safe. The survival of Arjuna was must for the survival of righteousness. He summed Ghatotkacha, the mighty son of Bhima in the battlefield. Ghatotakacha proved to be a cyclone for the entire Kaurava army. Duryodhana requested his friend

Karna to use his divine weapon that he had kept spare for his enemy Arjuna. With a great hesitation, he had to follow the command of his friend. He had no option but to use the weapon. He killed Ghatotakacha by this weapon. After this, the death of Karna became sure. If Ghatotakacha would have been summoned before this time, before the appointment of Karna as the commander of Kaurva army, the situation would have been different. It would have been the responsibility of the then commander of the Kaurava army to eliminate Ghatotkacha. Then, Karna would be safe and Arjuna would be in danger, righteousness would be in danger. So consideration of proper time and proper place is essential.

Lord Krishna understood Bhishma's Achilles heel. Bhishma wouldn't fight a woman. He summoned Shikhandi, a eunuch to fight with Bhishma. Bhishma was so orthodox in this context that he considered fighting a eunuch (He regarded a eunuch as a lady) was against the tradition of a brave person. He didn't face Shikhandi. Thus, Bhishma was eliminated from the battlefield.

A management person takes these factors into consideration and then proceeds.

Respect for Scriptures (Shastrachakshu)

Lord Krishna had always respect for ancient wisdom that was enshrined in scriptures. It is the collective knowledge and wisdom of our forefathers. They were so sacred that they were called divine. Here scriptures mean books of code of conduct. Each society has certain norms and codes of conduct. If the members of society don't follow the norms and conducts, there will be anarchy in the society. In modern age, there is constitution. People are guided by the constitution. A good citizen never goes against the constitution.

Similarly, to respect scriptures was the duty of all noble souls. Lord Krishna had a deep respect for the scriptures.

Pure (Shuchih)

Lord Krishna was an eternal abode of purity. He was able to purify others. Such a pure soul has eternal attraction. Purity is something beyond cleanliness. Cleanliness is an outer thing. Most of the people go to the extent of cleanliness only. But cleaning face and garments is not enough. Besides cleanliness, one needs purity. Purity is an inner attitude. Outer purity has effect, but temporary. Purity is related to heart. Those, who came into his close contact, could never leave him. There is no permanent effect of cleanliness. Purity comes through conscious effort. Meditation is one of the ways to achieve purity. Krishna was pure by birth.

A manager equipped with foresight strives to attain purity. Purity makes one's both worlds prosperous.

Control over Senses (Vashi)

Lord Krishna had control over all his senses. He couldn't be lured by any sort of lust. Someone is lured by carnal desire. Others are lured by power, prestige and money. To work with integrity and to succeed with integrity one needs control over his senses. Duryodhana was no control over his anger. He met his end. Keechaka had no control over his sexual desire. He was killed by Bhima, in his pursuit to lure Draupadi. Lord Krishna told innocent milkmaids of Braja to return from the rasa bhoomi. He permitted them to stay there only when they had no carnal desire. He was the chief strategist of the Mahabharata war. He could perform this difficult task only on the basis of his control of senses.

Six types of impurities are the cause of all most all the problems in the world, both at the individual and community levels. These are: uncontrolled sexual desire, anger, greed, lust, ego, jealousy etc. Lord Krishna had control over all these things. Those businessmen, who have control over their greed, invest in philanthropic activities. Earning much isn't a bad thing but sparing no space for anything except money in the life is a dangerous thing. This is greed. When money is earned through righteous ways, it gives a boost to economy. When it's earned through malpractices, it paralyses economy. A parallel economy (black money) emerges.

Patience (Sthirah)

Lord Krishna had highest level of patience. To conquer the trifles and to keep one's feet on terra firma one needs patience. Patience is maintained only when one has equanimity of mind.

It's an old saying—"Rome was not built in a day." Similarly success isn't a moment's game. To achieve success, one has to burn his midnight lamp. He could bear the separation from his parents for twelve years to kill the anti-social elements under the patronage of wicked king Kansa. He could bear the separation of his beloved Radha for the solving the problems of the world. Otherwise, who could wear such a separation?

We're aware of a famous hare and tortoise story. Hare was very fast. He had pride on his fastness. He challenged the tortoise to have a race with him. Tortoise had faith in his patience and continuous effort. He accepted the challenge. In the mid way, he undermined the tortoise's effort and fell asleep. The tortoise continued to move towards his target. The hare remained in his deep slumber but the tortoise reached the target. Patience with continuous effort bears the fruit.

A good manager doesn't outlet his reaction now and then. He waits for the right moment. But he doesn't allow the opportunity go in vain. He knows that time and tide waits for none.

Patience is an essential quality for achieving success.

Endurance (Dantah)

Endurance is a divine quality in for a qualified person, for a capable person, for a strong person. For the weak it's a problem. The weak can't bear any difficult situation. For endurance one needs both mental and physical strength. One may be physically strong but it's not necessary that he has a strong mind too. Some persons have strong mind but no strong body. To bear the fury of nature and to face man-made obstacles one needs both strong mind and body. Krishna had a both a strong mind and body. Due to his strength and skill, he is worshipped as the God incarnate. He was symbol of endurance. He didn't lose patience even before the most poisonous serpent, Kaliya. Tolerated its venom and came out from the jaw of death.

Forgiveness

Krishna forgave many sinners when they had repentance. He performed the worship of Govardhan instead of worshipping the king of gods, Indra. This made Indra furious. He was the rain god. He tried to deluge the entire Braja region under the spate of untimely rains. During this moment of crisis, Lord Krishna protected the Braja people. At last, Indra had to surrender.

Indra had committed a heinous crime. To satiate one's ego, harassing the innocent is a crime. People of Braja had no fault. They had to face the anger of Indra for no valid reason. Indra repented a lot. He came into the feet of Lord Krishna. He forgave him. To forgive is divine. If an individual comes through transformation, he is eligible for forgiveness. Indra underwent thorough transformation. Krishna forgave him.

A management person doesn't run after trifles. He forgives his colleagues as well as enemies for trifles.

Reserve (Gambhirah)

Lord Krishna wasn't a serious person. His integrity was respected everywhere. Being serious serves no purpose. On the other hand, it arouses aversion in peer group. Here, Hindi word 'gambir' isn't serious. It is reserve. Being reserve is one's right. At individual level as well as community level sometimes maintaining secrecy is needed. One should strike a balance between transparency and secrecy.

Lord Krishna's appearance and activities were always at a deeper level. No superfluous meaning could be drawn from those. He was a reserve personality. His used to disclose his intention only at the right moment.

He had knowledge of Karna's parentage. Kunti was his mother and the Sun god was his father. But Karna had no knowledge of his parentage. He was suffering all his life to know something about his real mother. Kunti was aware of the fact but he couldn't disclose it because of prevailing norms in the society. She had given birth to Karna when she was unmarried. If Krishna had disclosed the fact to Pandavas, they might not have fought the war. They would have surrendered their kingdom at the feet of Karna. On the other hand Karna was the friend of Duryodhana. He might have handed over the kingdom to Duryodhana. And hence the rule of wicked would be established. To destroy the wicked and to liberate the innocent was the mission of Krishna.

He revealed the fact when Pandavas were paying homage to his relatives slain during the Mahabharata war. Lord Krishna requested them to pay homage to Karna also. He wondered at his request. Then Lord revealed the fact that Karna was the eldest son of Kunti and to get a first and last homage from his younger brothers was his right. To get a due respect from juniors is a genuine thing. It's a good conduct. But supporting a wicked is against any ethics. Krishna didn't reveal the fact of Karna to Pandavas as long as Karna was fighting from the Kaurava side. After the death, performing last rites is the duty of family persons. Hence, Krishna reminded them to perform his duty.

Pandavas were very close to Krishna but he didn't reveal the reality about Karna till Karna's death. To maintain secrecy was the demand of the time. But when time came, he opened the lid of the cane. To be reserve means one needs a great digestive system. If one can't suppress some facts, one won't get success in his mission. When Indian scientists and defense personnel were proceeding towards Pokharan, a site for India's nuclear explosion experiment, they maintained secrecy. Even the intelligence services of the U.S.A. couldn't guess the modus operandi. Hence, personnel from India sides maintained secrecy.

But sometimes one needs to reveal something to make believe people. Lord Krishna revealed his cosmic form before Arjuna so that the latter could realise the truth. For realisation sometimes one needs revealing. Hence, there has to be a balance between secrecy and transparency.

Satisfied (Dhritiman)

Lord Krishna was satisfied. He was above the duality of life. Pleasure and pain, sorrow and misery couldn't affect his mental balance. Even in the situation of depression he didn't loose his temper. He never missed the touch of his tempo to achieve his mission. When his infant son Pradyumna was kidnapped, he didn't lose his balance but he ensured the safety of his son. Beating chest isn't the solution to any problem. For this one has to put endeavor in the proper direction.

When his sister's son Abhimanu was killed ruthlessly and by treachery, he didn't waste his time in weeping and crying. He wrote the death warrant for the main architect of this plot. He made proper arrangement for the end of Jayadratha.

A real yogi never gets disturbed by the duality of the world. He remains composed. A genuine management person should try to be a yogi. It doesn't mean that he should apathetic to pleasure and pain. He must be humane and playful but he should try to overcome depression caused by diurnal brouhaha.

Equality (Samah)

Human civilisation has been crying for equality since the historical phase. All most all great minds of the world irrespective of caste, creed, nation and community advocated the cause of equality. Krishna never differentiated friends and enemy. He tried his best to persuade even enemies of the society. But they were unwilling to move on the path of peace. They weren't ready to shun violence. Hence, Krishna had to stand by the side of truth. By his middle age he became famous all over Indian sub continent, yet he washed the feet of all the sages appeared in the sacrifice organised by the Pandvas. He was always above board.

A real management person shouldn't be a party in a petty affair unless it affects the health of his organisation as well as his personal honour.

A Great Donator (Danvirah)

Lord Krishna used to donate sometimes cows and wealth among needy persons. He never let anyone return empty hand from his house. His foster parents and own parents were also great donators.

Donation isn't promoting begging and laziness. Donation is a device to help the needy. In the society, due to certain reasons some people lag behind. They remain unable to cope with the dynamics of economic system. Their life remains static. To add mobility to their life, some sort of help is essential. Hence, donation is vital.

In most of the occasions, donation is properly utilised. Therefore, noble souls believe in philanthropic activities and they promote it.

Righteous (Dharmic)

Righteousness isn't imprisoned in the cave of a particular religion or a way of worship. The word 'dharma' isn't synonymous with religion. Dharma or righteousness is a way of living that is guided by one's conscience. Even a person without any affiliation to a particular religion may be righteous. Krishna lived a righteous life and determined his world with the lamp of righteousness. There is a chaos in all walks of modern life. The root of this chaos is absence of righteousness. People talk about emotional intelligence. It's good in some spheres. Goleman identified the five 'domains' of EQ (Emotional Quotient) as:

1. Knowing your emotions.
2. Managing your own emotions.
3. Motivating yourself.
4. Recognising and understanding other people's emotions.
5. Managing relationships, i.e., managing the emotions of others.

Despite inclusion of spiritualism in this EQ, one should apply righteous approach for long term personal prosperity as well as to make the entire community prosper. Lord Krishna became a part of the Mahabharata war only to root out evil elements dominant in the then Indian society. By this he established righteousness. Krishna loved only those people who had righteous heart.

Brave (Shoor)

Lord Krishna was a brave among the brave. Bravery demands internal strength more than external strength. Without external strength (physical strength) it's very difficult to overcome enemies. But mere possession of physical strength doesn't make one a brave person. Physical strength in association with the highest level of mind power makes one brave.

Arjuna was a mighty person. He was blessed with all sorts of sophisticated weapons available in the time. He was in the company of brave persons. He had best technologies, best weapons, mighty warriors and blessings of pious persons. But he wasn't ready to fight a decisive war against the wicked. To eliminate antisocial elements, it was essential to wage a war against the Kaurvas. Hence, at that point Arjuna needed tough mental support. There, at the battlefield of Kurukshetra, Lord Krishna delivered the sermon of the Gita. After understanding the message of the Gita, Arjuna got ready to fight the war.

Some people are born with great physical and mind power. Some labor hard to get it. Others don't strive to achieve such a wealth. Lord Krishna was always possessed with such powers. Arjuna's mind power was overshadowed by sentiments for a while. But under the guidance of a brave guru like Lord Krishna his weakness couldn't continue.

A brave leader understands the situation and doesn't allow weaknesses to hamper his task. On the basis of his endless bravery, he achieves his mission. **Only a brave can fulfill his mission.**

Sympathy (Karuna)

Sympathy is a divine quality. It makes a normal human being a saint. It's an essential human quality. Without sympathy, a man is nothing more than a clump of flesh and bones. The very fabric of human civilisation rests on sympathy.

Lord Krishna was always sympathetic to needy people. A deadly poisonous serpent was residing with his family members in the river Yamuna, near Mathura. He was causing pollution in the pure water of the river (during Lord Krishna's time, there were no industrial pollutants and other kinds of excreta in the Yamuna. Rivers were the life lines in Indian civilisation.) By drinking the polluted water of the river, many cattle and village people died. Krishna was very sympathetic to these innocent creatures. One day he jumped into the river, exactly on the very spot where Kaliya, the wicked serpent was residing and causing problems to the entire populace of the locality. He punished the serpent and forced him to leave the spot. In this way, Lord Krishna saved his community.

A genuine management person is possessed with the quality of sympathy; he helps his fellow men in the situation when they really need his help.

Respect for Elders/Seniors

All institutions depend on hierarchy. When the hierarchy works for progressive development of any institution, it makes the institution healthy. But when hierarchy is maintained only for hierarchy, it becomes a disease. Real noble persons, dignified persons, elders and seniors must be respected. Without this attribute, the very survival of any institution becomes difficult.

Krishna always respected his elders and seniors. On all important occasions he consulted his elders and seniors. But evil person like Kansa couldn't win his favour, despite being his close relative.

Respect is a matter of heart and a respected person gets respect. But whenever we come across an elder/senior, we should respect him/her because everyone's internal nature isn't written on his/her forehead. We vacate a seat in public transport, only due to this human quality. **Age and experience must be respected.**

Amiable (Saumyata)

You're an honest person. You're a hardworking fellow. You're intelligent too. You've good look. But you aren't amiable, so the chance of your success is minimal. In modern time, there's no dearth of intelligence. One can find hard working people. One can have an honest person, even though integrity has become one of the rarest qualities. First of all, to gauge one's personality, people see his amiable nature. It's in inborn quality. Sophistication is acquired but amiableness is the part of one's inner core. Hence, it's a great quality.

Lord Krishna was amiable in all his actions and behaviour. He had a smiling face. It wasn't like an artificial smile. He was full of eternal pleasure. To be a good manager, one needs amiable nature. If one is inborn amiable, he has this extra point. Lord Krishna was amiable not only in the company of his friends and girls in Vrindavan but he was equally amiable during the war of the Mahabharata.

One can be amiable only when one has a balanced personality. It's a great art. It's a meditation. One can't maintain his amiableness under compulsion or diplomacy.

Polite (Vinayi)

"He, who is down, need not fear falling." This isn't a bookish pronouncement of an English poet. It's core of behavioral contents. To achieve even a tough target one should be polite. A manager shouldn't be a person of hot temperament. During the moment of anger, a person looses his wit. To loose one's wit is a process of self annihilation.

During the war of the Mahabharata, Lord Krishna was from Pandavas side but he was behaving politely and respectfully with all the elders fighting from the side of the Kaurvas. To be polite even with enemies is a great art. A management person should have this art. This art should be applied even in the context when you've to take unpleasant and unpopular decision.

Hesitation in Listening Self-praise (Hriman)

A righteous person doesn't seek any entertainment in self-praise. He feels hesitation in listening self-praise. Lord Krishna was a living incarnation of righteousness. During his childhood, he performed many super human activities. He killed mighty demons. During his youth he helped many people. In all occasions beneficiaries praised Lord Krishna's deeds but he considered all his actions as parts of his duty. He was never influenced by his praise.

Praises boost a person. There's positive impact of praise on an individual but one shouldn't be swept by praise. A righteous person feels very hesitant in such a situation. To be influenced by self-praise is the act of shameful audacity.

Shelter to Refugee

Pandavas lost their common wife Draupadi in the game of gamble to Kaurvas. Duryodhana the eldest among Kaurvas ordered his younger brother Dushasana to pull Draupadi in the court, full of prestigious people of the time and make her nude. Pandavas had already lost his moral right to protest this decision. There was no one to help Draupadi. She requested many elders and brave persons present in the court to safeguard her modesty. But no help came from any corner. No one had guts to oppose Duryodhana and Dushasana. At last she started praying Lord Krishna. She said—"O Govinda, there's no one in this world to help a helpless lady like me, except you. Please come and safe guard my modesty. I'm in your shelter." Dushasana started pulling her sari and she closed her eyes. She continued to speak Lord Krishna's name. Wonder to all, Lord Krishna appeared there and started supplying sari. There was no end to the sari. At last Dushasana got tired and fell on the ground. Thus Draupadi's modesty was saved. Lord Krishna gave shelter to all those who took refuge in his feet.

A visionary manager forgives the mistakes of a genuine fellow and protects him. Such a gesture helps an individual to be cautious of repeating such a mistake. A decision may be wrong in a certain context, but intention must be genuine.

Ever Pleasant (Sukhi)

Pain and pleasure are the part and parcel of life. No one can deny this. But sorrow never touched Lord Krishna even once during his life time. His Gita sermon is a device to cure a person suffering from sorrow. Arjuna went deep into sorrow by the idea of killing his close enemies in the war waged to establish righteousness. He was swayed by emotion and overlooking his duty. Duty of a king is to uphold righteousness and protect his people. He shouldn't be influence by sentimental thoughts. Nothing is greater than performing one's duty on a righteous path. Krishna delivered Gita sermon to stop Arjuna from further deviation. His total effort was to free humanity from the yoke of sorrow. To achieve eternal peace of mind is the highest achievement in the life, particularly for those who understand the mystery of life. Lord Krishna was a great mystic. He propagated this idea of eternal peace through his Gita message. Without achieving eternal peace one can't be ever pleasant.

A good manager doesn't allow diurnal duality to over ride his personality. He commands such things and remains master of his personality.

Loving His Devotees (Bhakta Suhrita)

Lord Krishna was always taking care of his devotees. He could go to any extent to save his devotees. He fought with monsters and wicked kings to protect his devotees. He fought many wars for the sake of his devotees. His devotees were very righteous people. To uphold righteousness is one of the purposes of incarnations. Lord Vishnu fulfilled this purpose in all his incarnations. Lord Krishna is called the fullest manifestation of the Supreme Soul, the Lord Almighty. In India, particularly in Hinduism Lord Vishnu is regarded as Almighty, Supreme Soul. Lord Krishna was not only fighting wars for his devotees but fulfilling the righteous desire of his devotees.

When he was entering Mathura with an intention to kill Kansa, the wicked king, a hunched back lady wanted to see him and to apply sandal-wood paste on his forehead. Krishna understood her intention and deliberately came through the way the lady was passing. He accepted her offer. He touched her hunched back. With the delicate touch, a miracle happened. She became a beautiful lady with no hunched back. There're hundreds of such stories of Lord Krishna.

A genuine boss looks after his subordinates. He protects the interests of his fellows. A genuine boss commands respects of his subordinates. He always gets ready to take risks for the sake of his people.

Controlled by Love (Premvash)

Nothing could command Lord Krishna except love. He was under the control of his devotees. There's a permanent place of Radha in his heart. Krishna was always busy in many activities. It was very difficult to maintain all the relations. But never forgot any of his relations. Whenever any one talked about Radha, he went into deep meditation. He said—"Radha is my heart." Radha was his childhood love. He couldn't forget her in his whole life.

He couldn't forget Yashoda, her foster mother. His parents were in the prison of Mathura. He was brought up by Nanda and his wife, Yashoda. He never forgot his childhood friend Sudama and helped him when he was in a destitute position. His love was integral. In his love there was no distinction between beloved and lover. Both became one soul. A great poet of Maithili literature Vidyapati has said—

"Being always engrossed into the reminiscence of Krishna

Radha achieved oneness with him."

Lord Krishna practically showed the examples of his love. It wasn't on mental level only.

Welfare to All (Sarvashubhankar)

In the modern time, Mahatma Gandhi concluded from the book of Ruskin, "Unto the Last," that in the welfare to all lies in the welfare of an individual. Krishna in his Gita speech said—"To a wise man, there's no distinction between a supreme soul and an ant." There are always micros in macro.

In modern time, partial vision is the root of many problems. People think of the welfare of certain persons and certain segments. Our planners don't think of wider dimensions. An unspoken narrowness has overcast their intellect. They're wasting their all skills to solve the on going problems. They don't have integral vision. Nowadays, to save themselves from the meticulous long term planning, they talk about sustainable development. To achieve an environment of real sustainable development, they'll have to overcome their compartmentalised vision.

He didn't kill Kansa and his other wicked fellows to take his personal revenge. No one can achieve a great success on the basis his personal like and dislike. He worked for the welfare of the mankind. His each action had a message. These messages are for all time. Hence, they are eternal.

Valour with Competence (Pratapi)

His name was enough to create terror in the heart of wicked persons. After defeating and killing of Kansa, no king was willing to go against Krishna's campaign. All righteous persons started regarding him as the Lord Almighty. Those who was unwilling to move and determined to pose threats to innocent people had to perish. Being mighty is not enough. With might, one needs valour with competence.

People should know the deeds of a competent manager. Dr. A.P.J. Abdul Kalam designed missiles for India. People and the government recognised his work. He was offered the post of President of India. He accepted the offer and fulfilled the duty of the highest post with the same enthusiasm for which he was famous for.

Everyone in the time of Lord Krishna was stating, "There is righteousness where is Lord Krishna." He proved himself as the champion of truth. He had guts to work for truth and valor to fulfill his intention.

People invest in the name of such a manager. With dedicated work and integrity combined with integral vision make a name an epitome of reverence. To be such a manager needs a great sacrifice. Mr. Narayana Murthy worked with integrity and great discipline. He made his company Infosys a world class institution. After achieving such a height, he gave the charge of the company to the other competent fellow. Now he has become a source of inspiration for millions of people.

Fame (Karta)

Lord Krishna had a great fame in all directions of his contemporary world. This sort of fame wasn't achieved in a single moment. This was the result of a continuous and continual conscious effort in a right direction to make human life better. Those, who work in such a direction, earn real fame. We've hundreds of examples of selfless actions in all societies. Lord Krishna had no personal agenda. He had a mission. To work on a personal agenda isn't a necessarily bad thing. But it can't fetch the attention of the masses. Those, who work for the masses with no vested interest, earn spotless fame. Krishna never ruled any personal kingdom. He never enjoyed any fruit of his welfare activity.

People remember you not for what you receive but for the thing you give. Krishna gave the society much and took nothing. He continued to give. Those who think to give their organisation received naturally. Giving is important.

Affectionate by Nature (Raktalokah)

Lord Krishna was affectionate to most of the people. I don't say that he was affectionate to all. No one can be affectionate to wicked people. He wasn't affectionate to Kansa, Shakuni, Shishupal, Jarasandh and others because they were notorious people and they continued to harm mankind till their end. Even Jesus had enemies. He became victim of conspiracy. Gandhi had to sacrifice his life. So, one can be affectionate towards most of the people, not towards all of them.

A genuine management person has many fans and some enemies. He is affectionate to most of the people.

Lord Krishna was affectionate by nature. He drew attention of people from all walks of life towards him since his childhood.

This was only possible because he was affectionate by nature.

One can be affectionate by conscious practice also but being affectionate by nature is a great boon. It's a congenital blessing.

Shelter to Kind People (Sadhusamashrya)

Kind people could find refuge under the patronage of Lord Krishna. His doors were always open for such people. He gave shelter not only to kind people but other kind creatures also. He saved entire Brajabhoomi (the region known as Braja) from the fury of Indra, the king of gods. He gave shelter to Pandavas, driven out of their kingdom. He gave shelter to poor Sudama. He protected a mighty elephant from the deadly clutch of an alligator. He protected innocent subjects of Mathura from the continual attacks of Jarasandha.

A capable person should give patronage to kind people and help them to a maximum extent.

Winning the Heart of Women (Nariganmanohari)

Lord Krishna was very cute and loving. He was very handsome. Since his childhood he won the hearts of many beauties. There were many girl friends in his childhood. All of them had pure love for Krishna. Radha, Lalita and Vishakha were prominent among them. During his youth, he had eight wives. They were all beautiful ladies of their time. Lord Krishna took care of all of them. No one had any complain against him.

In modern times, polyandry and polygamy can't be in the vogue. But winning the heart of beauties is a great heart. To make one's beloved or wife happy in true sense is a great achievement. To lead a blissful marital life is a praiseworthy act for all ages. To respect ladies in home and in workplace is need of the hour.

Reverence for All (Sarva Aradhya)

Lord Krishna was revered by all. Bhishma and Dronacharya were fighting from Kaurvas' side but had all respect for Lord Krishna who was from opposite side. In Vrindavan, he was worshipped as the Supreme God. In Mathura and Dwarka, he was revered as the Almighty. In royal circle, he was regarded as an extraordinary charismatic personality. For Pandavas, he was the supreme master. They couldn't think or their existence without Krishna. Milk maid girls of Mathura led a life of prolong separation in his absence.

One should respect all. If you respect all, you will get respect from all. A genuine leader is revered by all.

Full of All-round Prosperity (Samridhiman)

Lord Krishna became synonymous to all round prosperity. His kingdom, Dwarka, was regarded as the source of wealth in his time. It was a port city. Trade and commerce flourished there. Lord Krishna's personality was full of auspicious qualities.

He himself led a life full of all round prosperity. By all round prosperity, we mean wealth with peace and pleasure. His wife (Rukmini) was regarded as the incarnation of Lama, goddess of wealth. During his childhood, he was brought up by a wealthy milk man, Nanda. His most of the friends were wealthy persons. He made his poor friend Sudama also a wealthy person.

One should try to make his entire circle wealthy. If your locality is full of wealthy and genuine fellows, naturally there will be peace and prosperity in your locality. In a prosperous community, a person leads a peaceful and pleasant life.

Greatness (Variya)

Lord Krishna was regarded as great among greatest persons. Saints and learned persons of his time regarded him as the greatest. When Yudhishthira called an assembly of kings, saints and learned persons of his time in his newly established kingdom, he asked his grandfather Bhishma—"Who should be offered first position ?" Bhishma answered his question immediately without any hesitation—"Where ever Lord Krishna is present, this question doesn't arise. Only he is capable to be offered the first position."

A great leader is offered first position by his people. He doesn't need to solve any equation to get first position. His greatness fetches all laurels naturally.

Almighty (God)

No one could disobey Lord Krishna. He achieved what he desired. Only God can do this. Even a mighty human being can desire. He can work hard to get his desired object. He can achieve success in getting many things but he can't achieve all things. Human beings have limitations. God is beyond any limitation.

This quality of Lord Krishna was supra-human. But one should try to excel in many arts and skills.

To be in One's Own Self (Sada Swarup Samprupta)

Lord Krishna was uninfluenced by any sort of illusion. He was always in himself. He was a living example of self control. Self control is great achievement. Before controlling others, one needs to control oneself.

People move to win the world but they've no self control. Ultimately, their campaign doesn't reach the target. Their dream remains unfulfilled. Hence, they feel defeated.

To be in self control, one needs to be in oneself. To be in one self, one needs to understand his personality. There're many layers of dirt and dust on our inner self. To make it clean, one needs to clean all the layers on our personality. Some layers are imposed by family, some by society and some by one's own acts and thoughts.

Omniscient (Sarvagya)

Many people can know many things. Some people can know most of the things but one can't be omniscient. We've already talked of human limitation. Lord Krishna was omniscient. This was his super human quality. Only God can be omniscient. A human being can't be omniscient. A man can know many things. He can be a scholar, a genius but he can't be omniscient.

One should try to learn many things. One should strive hard to get all round exposure but being omniscient is beyond the limit of human being.

Ever New (Nitya Nootan)

Novelty was the main feature of Lord Krishna's personality. This aspect was the main source of attraction in his personality. There was no chance of monotony in his company.

To be always in the centre stage, one needs an ever novelty in his personality.

A great leader is always innovative. Innovation is the motto to remain at the helm of affair. Without innovation one can't taste the fruit of novelty. Without novelty one can't survive for a long period.

Innovation is the motto and novelty is the mantra to be a management guru.

Divine Incarnation (Sachhidanada Vigraha)

Lord Krishna was a divine incarnation. One can put effort to achieve some sort of divinity but one can't be a divine incarnation.

Divinity in thought is possible but divinity in entire body constituent isn't possible. This quality can't be achieved through any art and craft or even through meditation.

Master of All Skills (Sarva Siddhi)

We've heard of many yogis who had extraordinary powers. But a human being can't be master of all skills. Lord Krishna possessed all most all yogic powers. He was the master of all skills. For a human being, it's impossible to be master of all powers and skills.

A leader should try to possess many sorts of skills and powers. This can be from mind power to strong body. One can have a strong mind and a strong body.

A Power beyond Cosmic Laws (Avachintya Mahashakti)

Lord Krishna had power to go beyond cosmic laws. He overshadowed the sun. All warriors in the war of Mahabharata came under the illusion that it was sunset. Arjuna had taken a vow to kill Jayadratha before sunset; otherwise he would burn himself to death in the pyre. Believing the onset of the sunset, Jayadratha came to see Arjuna jumping into the fire pit but suddenly the sun started shining in the sky. It was noon. Lord Krishna ordered Arjuna to kill the wicked Jayadratha immediately without wasting a single moment. And he did so. No human being can go against the cosmic order. Only He can go.

Cosmic Form (Koti Brahmand Vigraha)

Lord Krishna blessed Arjuna to see his cosmic form, just before the war of the Mahabharata. He saw many universes in the body of Lord Krishna. It's not possible for human beings. This isn't possible even through miracles. Hence, it's not for inspiration. It's for information only.

A leader should be charismatic instead.

Base of All Incarnations (Avatarvali Bijam)

Lord Krishna wasn't an incarnation only. He was the sum total of all incarnations. All incarnations spring up from his cosmic body. He is the base of all incarnations.

His multi-dimensional personality, cosmic forms, divine acts, miracles, yogic power, valour, smartness and many other qualities support this statement.

Bliss to Enemies Killed by Him (Hatargatidayak)

Lord Krishna gave bliss to all the persons killed by him. At the last moment such wicked persons understood Lord Krishna's divine form and achieved bliss (Moksha). Understanding of truth is bliss in itself. By understanding the truth in their last moments, even wicked persons attained bliss.

Centre of Attraction for Those Who Had Attained Bliss (Atmaramganakarshi)

He was the center of attraction for all those who attained bliss. He is called king of yogis. A righteous person becomes the center of attraction for all. Lord Krishna was the very source of righteousness. He was full of divine qualities.

We get respect for our qualities. One can get respect from

his staffs and subordinates but it'll of very temporary nature. To command a real respect one needs good qualities full of humane sentiments and kindness. Getting this sort of respect is a great achievement. To be revered by great persons is the greatest achievement.

Wonderful Miracles (Sarvadbhuta Leela)

Lord Krishna performed wonderful miracles during his life time. This sort of action is beyond the reach of human being. One can wonder at such things.

A leader can be charismatic. He can perform some extra ordinary roles. He can cross some mile stones. His followers can be inspired by his extraordinary intellect.

Incomparable Sweetness (Atulya Madhurya)

His sweetness had no comparison. All saints, ascetics, ladies from villages, gopis, kings and princes were attracted by his sweetness. It was eternal.

In a normal sense, sweetness is the nectar of one's personality. On the basis of sweetness, many people achieve success.

Sweetness is the first step to success. A leader must possess sweetness in his personality. Lord Krishna had everlasting sweetness. Hence, it was incomparable.

Attracted All the Three Worlds by His Flute Recital (Murali Swar Se Tino Lok Vijay)

Lord Krishna was the master of music and dance. He was very much attracted towards flute recital. Whenever he had time, he used to recite flute. Even during the war of the Mahabharata, he used to keep flute with himself. He was so much fond of his flute that he didn't give it even to Radha, his beloved, despite her request.

Knowledge of music becomes an attraction in one's personality. A leader should take interest in arts, music and cultural activities. Even multi-national companies organise music concerts. They promote art and cultures. **This is called business with an aesthetic sense.**

Exceptionally Handsome (Asadharan Rupalavanya)

Lord Krishna was extraordinarily handsome. All the creatures of the world were hypnotised by his tenderness, delicacy and beauty.

A beautiful face is really a gift of god. It attracts many persons. Even a wicked person gets attracted by the charm of beauty. There are instances in human history that kings relinquished their crowns for the sake of beauty.

Lord Krishna's smartness and charm had universal appeal.

Out of these sixty four attributes most of can be found in human beings but some of the qualities can essentially be found in God. We human beings can be inspired by some of qualities of Lord Krishna in different formats as per the need of the time. Some of these qualities can be developed inside by conscious effort but some are inborn. I think a brief sketch of sixty four attributes in the personality of Lord Krishna can be informative and helpful for all those who aspire to excel in any field in their life.

Part II

Lord Krishna and Management at Organisational Level

3. Understanding the Organisation

वदन्ति तत्तत्त्वविदस्तत्त्वं यज्ज्ञानमद्वयम्।
ब्रह्मेति परमात्मेति भगवानिति शब्द्यते॥

- श्रीमद्भागवत

Vadanti Tattatvavidastavam yajgyanmadwayam
Brahameti Parmatameti Bhagavniti shabadyate

– *From* ***'Shrimadbhagvata'***

Meaning: *People try to realize the truth through different ways. All the ways are same. Lord is called by brahma , parmatma and bhagvan. Different ways of realization merge at one point.*

Human mind is a treasure of most precious jewels of this world. But it's also a vast ocean of poisons. Here words are simple but they're metaphors.

One has to employ certain connotations and denotations to decode metaphors. In a similar way, we can understand the place value of 'jewels' and 'poisons.' Here, these words have no face value, they've place value only.

In computer technology, we come across the 'GIGO' factor. Life is not so much mechanical. Neither it's so much scientific. We don't have a complete artistic life as well. It's an amalgamation of many 'ifs' and 'buts.' There are many pluses and minuses in our life. For a surrealist, life is full of thorns.

There is no beauty in life. No juice of human kindness flows out of it. For an idealist, life is a bed of roses. For a mechanical person, life is a bundle of facts and figures. None of the three is near to truth. Life is a science, it's an art, it's commerce and it's more than anything that can be defined by any technical term. After all, it remains an enigma, a puzzle. But a careful and intelligent individual solves this puzzle to the maximum extent.

First step in this direction is understanding. Understanding of a problem is the solution of the problem. How can we understand?

The methodology of understanding is to understand "what is." Often, we overlook "what is," We not only overlook "what is," but also deny it sometimes. We sometimes escape from "what is." Why not? Escapism is very easy. At least it seems so. But it's the cause of many ills. It's not so easy to escape. Your life is always with you.

Before clarifying above propositions and dealing with the topic, let me put some more propositions.

Generally, we perceive our life as the part of our physical existence. But here, '6' is '9.' It's not a complete reverse case. It's like the cocktail of water image and mirror image ....of our perception. Here, I would like to say that an individual is the part of his life. Seems queer? Isn't that so? Prima facie? ......Yes. But digging deeper. Then ...no.

We have a life. It's a grand total of many things. There are many determinants in life. Some of them may be summarised as:

- A society in which we're born
- Parentage
- Upbringing
- Individuality
- Friendship during childhood and adolescence
- literature/art/craft
- Overall exposure

- Goals and ideals
- Circumstances

Besides, the above factors there're many things. If the percentage of negativity is higher in some or most of the above determinants, personality of an individual bears negative traits. Here, we understand the utility of 'GIGO' i.e. garbage in and garbage out. A higher proportion of garbage, a higher percentage of negativity, an increased frequency of minuses in a person makes one's mind a vast ocean of poisons. This vast ocean doesn't lie in a pacific stage always. With the slight movement of wind tides become visible. The person starts showing negativity. His personality becomes a garbage house and it stinks now and then.

Similarly, if the percentage of positive things and pluses of the above determinants remains higher in a person he shows positive tendencies. His behavior becomes positive and inspiring. His mind becomes a treasure of the most precious jewels of the world. He becomes a scientist. An artist. An actor. A sports person. A successful businessman (rather a businessman interested in other's welfare also). And so on....... And above all, a good human being.

But an individual isn't solely responsible for his personality or his life. He has control over certain things, but not on all determinants. No doubt, with his deliberate effort he can change his himself. Hence, what we've is the *summum* bonum of many determinants. We're responsible for some, not all. It's not in our control. Hence, human life isn't a part of his physical existence. Hence, our life is beyond our physical existence Now what we can do ?We can put our endeavor to subside negativity and fill up the tumbler with positive elements, nectar that is spread on this beautiful earth(Though it's not evenly spread). It helps us in all walks of life.

On account of overflowing negativity inside and outside, we don't see "what is." Often we see "what isn't" or "what should be." Perceiving "what isn't" instead of "what is," makes our eyes jaundiced. After understanding "what is," we can deliberate on "what should be." It's the next step.

For understanding of "what is," one has to practice a lot. Some people say (like Lord Krishna, Buddha, Osho, J. Krishnamurthy...) it's a process of meditation. Others say it's a practice to see a thing without being prejudiced. Both are the same thing. Prejudices and meditation don't go together. A mind without prejudices is a meditative mind. A mind able to see "what is."

Is it possible to lead a life without prejudices imposed by many determinants life of the past? Though it's difficult, it is possible. Lord Krishna has made it possible. And we can make it happen too.

An organisation has many components—man (Human resources), material (infrastructure—financial, technological, access to market) and something more. These are the coarse fabrics of a body that is known as an organisation. But the goal of an organisation is the fine muslin for its body. Location of the organisation (though location in the age of communication may be defined in a different way, its importance can't be denied) is the runway for its flight. But the motto of the organisation is the soul of the organisation. Unfortunately, parties playing for mere profit have no motto. No matter, what is there and what isn't.

If you're able to see the one facet of a coin, you'll be able to see the other facet without much difficulty. Understanding "what is" is the most important thing.

Understanding of "What is" gives one a sense to understand "What isn't there."

There's no grand finale in the life. There's no last point. There's no highest peak. There's no Mount Everest. After an ascending, there's a descending. The moon passes through waxing phase in a fortnight and she moves through waning phase in another fortnight. It's neither concrete, nor abstract. But it's something between the two. It's something beyond the two. It's a flux.

To make your vision clear, you'll need a powerful retina. You'll have to purify your jaundiced eyes because everything looks yellow to a jaundiced eye. You'll have to overcome prejudices. To overcome prejudices, you'll have to forget the hang ups of your past. It's very difficult. Sweet memories of the past make us nostalgic but the bitter memories of the past continue to haunt us. Here you can't escape from them. Escapism isn't the answer.

An organisation appoints a person on the basis of his talent, qualification and experiences. Without going into the past how can we judge any one's experience? For employing our experience, we go into our past. Without learning the driving, it's impossible to drive. When we drive, we concentrate on the way i.e. on the present. But this concentration on the present is the result of our meticulous effort of the past. Therefore, skillful employment of the past is an art for the betterment of the present. But to drive in the present, you need a concentration. Hang up, prejudice, negativity and minuses (here, minuses means "thinking of our shortcomings and the goals that we couldn't achieve in our life") form garbage in our mind. This garbage makes our eyes jaundiced.

With our conscious effort we can clear the garbage that has been dumped into our mind by the society, religion, parentage, circumstances, faulty education system, our carelessness and many such things. The day we start looking at "what is," we'll be able to understand our organisation. Once we achieve expertise in watching "What is," we'll be more playful. We'll understand our organisation in its genuine form. We can understand the expectations of our boss, feelings of our subordinates, intensions of our colleagues and inside-outside grape vines. A man having such an understanding will rule the roost. Lord Krishna had such an understanding.

An employ is thrown out of an organisation because he hasn't understood his organisation. Sometimes the modus operandi of an organisation or a boss doesn't suit an employee and he himself relinquishes the organisation. Self decision is also the result of understanding. Lack of understanding is the cause of many organisational ills.

Life of Krishna is an inspiring encyclopedia for understanding. Here are some of the fragments from it.

Krishna had to face many odds in his life. But he had the highest order of receptivity. His senses very sharp.

He was born in a prison. His parents were put behind bars, not for any criminal offence but for their goodness. Krishna's maternal uncle Kansa, the king of Mathura had a firm belief in a prophecy that the eighth son of Devaki would kill him. He was so much afraid that he put Devaki and her husband (Vasudeva) behind bars so that he could kill the new born baby of Devaki. Incidentally, (Vasudeva) managed to keep the boy for his further security in Gokul where his friend Nand rai was living.

There're many stories interwoven around Krishna's character. Kansa sent Putana, a dreaded demon to kill the new born baby. She disguised herself as a lady from Gokul. She took the boy in her lap and started feeding him her breast. But boy was intelligent enough to understand that they were not familiar breasts; they weren't of his mother. This understanding made him aware of her intension. Because of this understanding Krishna could save his life. **Proper understanding is the first step to protection and prosperity.** It's quite usual that even a toddler, having no exposure to any experience can feel touch of his mother and distinguish it from other lady. It reflects the fact that Krishna had a developed sense of touch even in his childhood.

During his childhood phase he killed many demons sent by Kansa. He had understood the nature of unexpected events. The survival instinct became intense in him. He had to face so many odds in his early years that people had to believe in his extraordinary caliber and he was recognised as the complete manifestation of the supreme soul, divinity. This faculty made him mature enough to enjoy war and love with equal ease. Even in the company of beautiful girls of Braja he didn't loose his balance. He could kill Kansa because he understood his power, wealth, army and people's reaction against him. During intermittent attack on Krishna by Kansa's devil attendants, a volley of reaction against the terror of Kansa was accumulated. Krishna understood his own strength, he became aware of his enemies weakness and strength, and he felt the love and emotion of people and then waged a war against the enemy of society. Despite lack of adequate means the Pandavas could fight a deciding battle against the Kaurvas. This was because of an omnipotent presence of Lord Krishna. **A man of understanding is more powerful then an army of fools. Because in a decisive battle, mind wins and mindless loses.**

For proper understanding one needs clarity and an enhanced level of senses. Krishna had a developed sensuous faculty. He employed his past experiences skillfully to excel in the present. No hang up. Therefore, he could experience victory in the all walks of life.

For understanding one should follow these points as Lord Krishna did (one shouldn't feel that one has supernatural capacity like Krishna). One should read the inherent message hidden in between lines of his acts:

- Use past experiences for the betterment of present.
- No hang-up.
- Look an object without prejudice.
- After looking try to grasp the gist of the object.
- Then compare the object with other things.
- After comparison feel other's point of view regarding the object.
- Judge but don't be judgmental.
- Is useful to you what image you've built of the object in your mind?
- First watch what is going on. Is it correct?
- Any change is expected from you?
- Are you in a position to change anything?
- Before understanding of any object/organisation,

you need to understand yourself.

- You need to understand the depth of a pond only to swim without any hurdle. Gauzing depth isn't your goal.
- Understanding is essential only to work smoothly and excel in the set up. Understanding is means, not an end.
- To achieve a better end, you need a better means. Hence, understanding.

4. Fixing the Goal

अन्तवन्त इमे देहा नित्यस्योक्ताः शरीरिणः।
अनाशिनोऽप्रमेयस्य तस्माद्युध्यस्व भारत॥

– *श्रीमद्भगवद्गीता*

Antavanta eme deha nityasyoktah sharirinah
Anasinoaprameyasya tasmadyudhasva bharata

– *From* ***'Shrimad bhagavadGeeta'***

***Meaning**: The destruction this body tha carries the immortal, infinite and eternal soul is sure. Hence fight to achieve your goal.*

It's mentioned no where that Krishna ever pronounced his goal. His deeds reflected that he pursed the path to establish righteousness and eliminate those who were posing threat to saints and innocents and to those who were dangerous to the very existence of righteousness. On the basis of such deeds he is called the complete incarnation of Lord Vishnu. Vishnu is the supreme God in Hindu Pantheon who is in charge of establishing order in the entire cosmos.

It's an obvious fact that Great Masters have no personal goal in their life. They've overcome their personal needs and wants. If you've no material need, no want, you are a Master. Such masters have only mission. The core content of their mission always remains betterment of human society.

In his mission to establish social order, he had to face many antisocial elements.

To save other, one needs to protect oneself first. Krishna understood the very fact in his early life that without eliminated the anti social elements, social order can't be established. First step in this direction was to protect oneself. Protecting oneself from all odds is the first major step in the direction of proving oneself. He protected himself and his men from the onslaught of demons. Who were these demons? They were attendants of Kansa.

They were expert in the art of disguising themselves and hurt people in disguise. Such elements are found in all ages. Sometimes under the influence of a particular despot or sometimes under the influence of a particular ideology such elements harass innocent people.

At organisational level many unexpected hurdles appear. Sometimes bottleneck posed by some opponents or competitors. They may be from inside the organisation or from outside. Without tackling such elements, without neutralising their influence, it's quite impossible to make any further movement. While tackling such elements one has to look after the smooth functioning of his organisation. Without smooth functioning of your organisation, without profit you can't tackle your opponents, you can't defeat your enemy. **Only a strong person/organisation can face competition. Only a mighty can win the race**.

Before the identification of hurdles, one needs to identify one's goal. There're many options in human life. There're many sorts of career opportunities before young men. There're choices before an organisation. There're many attractive assignments to lure an individual. But it depends on the individual to choose the most appropriate goal. Here I'm not talking about the best or the worst goal because goal is comparative concept. It varies according to person, place or situation. It depends on an individual or in case of an organisation it depends on decision maker/makers/board of directors to select a goal. If you're manufacturing warm clothes, your target group will be from the countries which are cold prone. You can't supply your product to South African people where climate is extremely hot. If you're releasing a magazine on astrology your potential clients won't be from Islamic world because in Islam doesn't believe in astrological impact on human beings. So goal varies according to place, ideology, person and situation. A staunch believer in Islam can't choose a profession of lending money on interest. Some people want to make money but they've certain ethical ideas, so they can't make money where protection of such ideas is essential.

Some people want to invest money but they're afraid of investing in stock market. They want to play safe game. They want to invest in real estate.

They don't run like a hare, they want to move like a tortoise. But ways have pluses and minuses. But no play is quite safe, especially up to the degree you expect it to be safe. There's no achievement without risk. **Risk brings a romance in life. If you no the art of swimming a pond is always a source of enjoyment and merry making in your life. If you've no such skill, a pond will always remain a fearsome spot for you. An experienced sailor predicts the arrival of typhoon much before its onset. He manages accordingly.**

Before fixing your goal, you need to understand yourself. To understand yourself you shouldn't be driven by desire. Before moving in the direction of your desire, you need to put your feet on a firm base. During the time of Krishna, many kings in the Indian subcontinent were trying to mold the polity of the region as per their whims and fancies. They had to appropriate goal. What to talk of mission.

Goal is personal. It may be of temporary nature or be of permanent. Target is associated with a particular project or product or assignment. Mission is eternal. It may have certain personal nuances but it's always associated with a wider perspective.

Krishna had a mission. It wasn't driven by any whims and fancy. The motto of his mission was to eliminate the wicked and to establish a better world order. To pursue such a wider goal, one needs many qualities. Besides, strength, intelligence, diplomacy, bona fide intention, excellence in the art of warfare, persuasive quality, amiable personality, sense of time and situation, art to influence people, hard labor, objectivity one needs to fulfill the demand of the time. Krishna had all these qualities. On the basis of such qualities he could set his mission.

5. Options for Attaining the Goal

नियतं कुरु कर्म त्वं कर्म ज्यायो ह्यकर्मणः।
शरीरयात्रापि च ते न प्रसिद्ध्येदकर्मणः॥

– श्रीमद्भगवद्गीता

Niyatam kuru karma tvam karma jyayo hyakarmah
Shariryatrapi cha te na prasidhyedkarmanah

– *From **'shrimadbagavadgeeta'***

Meaning: *Do the work you have already determined because doing work is better than doing nothing. Without action even the existence of your body isn't possible.*

It's always a wise step to consider options before taking a decision to attain goal. Goal is achieved through a long term strategy but target is time bond. To fulfill the goal, one has to achieve target regularly.

It's very difficult to change decision often. To change decision often affects one's entire set up. Therefore one should select option. Sometime, there may be some variations in achieving goal and target but it shouldn't be completely contradictory.

One, who thinks big, grows big. Setting up a goal is the prolong outcome of a high thinking. Generally people have targets. But there is nothing wrong in setting up targets only. People have different levels.

Krishna always contemplated options to achieve his goal. There was no contradiction between his target and goal. It seems that for him life was an integral flow. Despite waxing and waning phases in life, he was always in a composed state. Despite his logical faculty, his life was rhythmical. There is a rhythm in a balanced life.

Krishna was leading a normal life. He was playing with his friends, enjoying the company of girls and doing almost all good activities. But wicked forces were intervening in his life. He had no personal target, no such goal.

For the society, he killed demons. For the society, he fought many battles. He dedicated his life to the mankind. Kansa wasn't the only demon dangerous for the society. He had thousands of evil associates who were inflicting terror on the innocent. To relieve society from the spate of their terror, it was necessary to end the reign of terror.

To end the reign of Kansa was his goal in childhood. To achieve this goal, he had targets. Killing Putna, Bakasura, Mustik, Chanur and other demons was his aim. There was a nexus between all evil elements present in the then India. To break the nexus, he had to align all the anti terror forces. Jarasandha, Shishupal, Dantavaktra, Duryaodhana and Shakuni were birds of the same feather. Krishna had to give a death blow to all these elements.

He fought some duels, battles etc. to eliminate them. Sometimes, he inspired other warriors like Bhima to kill evil persons like Jarasandha. To achieve your mission you need time to think, you need space for yourself. He shifted along with his close relatives from Mathura to Dwarka. One shouldn't perish one's potential in skirmishes.

After the death of Kansa, his father-in-law, Jarasandha was burning with anger to take revenge. He was attacking Mathura now and then. To save its innocent subjects from the onslaught of Jarasandha and to fulfill his mission, he left Mathura and made Dwarka his kingdom. All his kith and kin supported him in his endeavor. From this point he inspired others to annihilate such elements. Jarasandha was killed during the Rajsuya Sacrifice (a sacrifice performed by kings) by Bhima. People like Shakuni and Duryodhana were killed during Mahabharata war.

Those who support criminals shouldn't get any safe passage. Bhishma and Dronacharya were good people but they supported the Kaurvas during the War. Krishna respected the merits of Bhishma and Dronacharya but they stood on the wrong side.

In human life one can have many options. In many options, choice becomes difficult. But in a single option, there's no choice. Choice is determined by the target. But one select a righteous way attain a righteous target. To reach a pure end, one should follow the righteous means. Otherwise long time survival becomes difficult.

In quick success, there may be attraction. A daffodil has much attraction. But its life span is very short. Hence, it can't be a source of attraction for a leader. There's no future prospect of leadership without stability. A leader has to control many emotions to achieve his target. Despite the good nature of Bhishma and Dronacharya, Lord Krishna had no hesitation in employing devices to kill them because they were in the wrong side. They were with a lost cause. Their deeds would be against the human civilisation. **Hence, choice must be in the direction of achieving target.**

6. As You Sow, So You Reap

किं कर्म किमकर्मेति कवयोऽप्यत्र मोहिताः।
तत्ते कर्म प्रवक्ष्यामि यज्ज्ञात्वा मोक्ष्यसेऽशुभात्॥

- गीता

Kim karma kimkarmeti kavyoapyatra mohitah
Tatta karma pravakshyami yajgyatva
mokshyayaseshubhat

- From ***'The Geeta'***

Meaning*: Even wise persons are confused in deciding what is action and what is inaction. I'll teach you and with the help of my teaching you'll be relieved from all the negative influences.*

In this book, I've never mentioned a fact—"Why was the War of the Mahabharata fought?" This question demands some sentences to satisfy the query of those who're not so much aware of Indian culture. It's said—"All most all ideas are in a single book and this is the Mahabharata." I think this sort of tall claim wasn't put forward, at least by the author of the book. It's a statement put forward by an impressed critic and passed from generations to generations. But one can't deny the vivid pictures of life depicted in the book.

Originally, it's a story of Kuru clan who ruled over Hastinapura, an important kingdom in ancient India for centuries. With this story, many other stories are interwoven. Of course, story of Lord Krishna finds the most important berth in the book. There're descriptions of many small scale wars in the book. But the most destructive war was fought between the Kaurvas and the Pandavas. Lord Krishna didn't fight from any side but he was the chief strategist from Pandavas' side. Besides this he was the charioteer of Arjuna.

Kaurvas were the sons of Dhritrashtra and Pandavas were the sons of Pandu. Dhritarashtra and Pandu were brothers. Dhritrashtra, the elder brother was blind by birth. For his blindness, his claim to the crown was denied. His younger brother, Pandu, was crowned as the king of Hastinapura. Though he had love for his brother but he couldn't hide his feeling to be the king.

Pandu ruled his kingdom with a righteous approach. He was a great warrior. He fought many wars and expanded the boundary of his kingdom. Subjects had a great respect for his king. But the destiny had a different a plan. One day he was on a hunt mission. By mistake, his arrow struck in the heart of a sage who in a love making gesture with his wife. In fact, the sage took the form of a deer and his wife took the same guise. They were deeply involved in. The king thought that a deer was playing. He saw the point from a distance. But the sage was in indulged in the act with a great intensity. He wasn't aware of his outside world. When he was lost in love making, an arrow struck his heart. It took his life. Before his death, he gave a curse to Pandu—"Whenever you'll come close to your wife, you'll die in the extreme moment of passion."

Pandu was a righteous person. He accepted his fault and went into deep sorrow. In the condition of repentance, he returned to his kingdom. He handed over his kingdom to his brother as his viceroy and went to forest with his two wives and five sons. In the forest life was going smoothly. But with the passage of time, he forgot the curse and went closer to his second wife, Madri. It proved fatal to him. He lost his life. Madri burnt herself alive in the pyre of her husband. Having lost everything, the elder queen Kunti returned to Hastinapur with her five minor sons.

After the death of Pandu, Dhritrashtra grabbed the throne to fulfill his long cherished desire. He had hundred sons. All were known as Kaurvas. Duryodhana was eldest among them but he was younger than Yudhishthira, the eldest among Pandavas. Yudhishthira had a natural claim to the throne but Dhritrashtra was unwilling to accept his claim. To deny him the crown, he started playing tricks.

Dignified persons of the time associated with the court of Hastinapura favoured Yudhishthira but they didn't oppose Dhritrashtra's lustful decision in a conclusive tone. Duryuodhana, having found the favour of his father and maternal uncle Shakuni started torturing Pandavas in different ways from an attempt to burn them alive to defeating and taking away their kingdom and entire possession in gambling.

At last, to end their saga of suffering, they decided to get their kingdom through an amicable solution but Duryodhana was made up of a different stuff. He was a mere representative of Dhritarashtra's uncontrolled ambition. He wasn't ready to return even an inch of land to the Pandavas. Lord Krishna tried his best to persuade Duryodhana. But contrary to the honour of an ambassador he tried to imprison the Lord Krishna. He couldn't do so. Thus, the war of the Mahabharata was fought. In this war, the entire Kaurava clan was annihilated. Hence, as you sow, so you reap.

"Don't let this opportunity go. Life is short, time is fleeting. Time and tide wait for none. Strike the iron while it is hot." Generally, people don't comprehend the real intention behind such sayings. They distort the surface under the water as per their present need. No doubt, one should take care of his present need but fulfilling the need by hook and crook poses threat to the subject in the long run. If you cheat some one, you harm him for the time being but you've to move on a wrong track. It is very difficult to opt for a wrong track once and leaving this path instantly.

In this context, we've a lot of examples. These examples can be sited from the life of Lord Krishna, from the lives of his devotees, from the war of the Mahabharata and from modern corporate sector. In modern time, Mahatma Gandhi had worked on this principle. He decided to fight the freedom struggle of India by the weapons of truth and non-violence. Behind this decision, there was a deeper meaning. Kings used to establish their states through the might of weapons. In the state craft, might is right. The strong capture the weak. The former ruled over the latter. The basis foundation of state rests on blood and treachery. Gandhi wanted to alter this equation. He wanted to make India a nation where there will be no exploitation. It was possible only through proceeding on the path of truth and non-violence. Moving through a wrong track one can't reach a destination of truth. It doesn't mean that Gandhi was a sentimental idealist who was in search of a Utopia. He was aware of the statecraft. He was very much aware of the people's nature. He had to face many wicked persons in his life. His non-violence wasn't an escape from the practical situation. It wasn't asceticism. But it was a conscious effort to recognize' cause and effect' theory. You should get ready to reap what you've sown.

The entire Kaurava clan was killed. Lord Krishna was well aware of the very fact of the life—"As you sow, so shall you reap." When Karna was going to fulfill the conditions laid down in the Swayamvar of Draupadi, Lord Krishna hinted Draupadi to object Karna. She followed the dictate. Some scholars blame Krishna's this act as partial. But he was aware of Karna's nature. Karna was in the company of Duryodhana and his friend. Personally Karna was a man of character but he was in the company of wicked persons. He had no guts to oppose Duryodhana and party. Krishna was expecting something more from Draupadi. She should be the part of his mission to establish the reign of righteous person. Pandavas were the emblem of righteousness in India. Hence, he inspired hinted Arjuna to fulfill the condition.

We should think twice before a major action. Had Draupadi been married to Karna, the history of India would have been completely different. Hence, Krishna gives the message of purity in action through his life and the sermon of the Gita.

7. Extra Factors and Risk Management

हतो वा प्राप्यस्यसि स्वर्गं जित्वा वा भोक्ष्यसे महीम्।
तस्मादुत्तिष्ठ कौन्तेय युद्धाय कृतनिश्चयः॥

– *गीता*

Hato va prapyasyasi swargam jitva va bhokshyase mahim
Tasmaduttishtha Kaunteya Yudhaya Kritnishchayah)

– *From* **'Geeta'**

***Meaning**: O son of Kunti, if you meet your death in this battle , you'll find your place in Heaven but if you win , you'll enjoy the crown in this world. Hence , stand fight.*

Boldness without being cautious is a fool's intelligence. Only a cautious person takes extra factors into consideration. There's an extra factor in all walks of life.

Kaurvas were mighty and brave like Pandavas. They were only brave persons. Karna was a great warrior. Shakuni was a cunning person. Being cunning spoils one's self image. One should be a strategist. Lord Krishna was a real strategist. He was aware of all extra factors to come into the way of Pandavas. He had already developed strategy to face those factors. He had employed all skills for risk management.

Recently a mega wave destroyed lives and resources in the coastal area of Japan. It damaged severely many nuclear reactors of Japan. Japan tried it's best to minimise the danger. It rose after the situation. Had it developed strategy to face extra factors, it could manage the risk. It was a case in Japan. What to talk of developing nations?

There're a lot of natural and financial crisis in our personal, organisational and national life. At various levels, we observe that people don't have proper arrangement to face risk. They start searching remedies in the time of crisis. We don't get result most of the time as per our expectation. Hence, we need emotional guts to face the consequences which may be contrary to our expectation.

Krishna always took care of extra factors and was ready to work in the moment of crisis. A good planer thinks ahead. He has future plans. He is expert in crisis management.

After the brutal killing of Arjuna's son (Abhimanyu) in the battlefield. Arjuna took a vow to kill the main conspirator (Jayadratha) by the next evening otherwise he decided to jump into a pyre to immolate himself. He took oath but didn't have any strategy to kill Jayadratha except his bravery. Usually, in such a situation any won't come out. Because in his absence he'll enjoy victory. If Arjuna hadn't found Jayadratha, he would commit suicide. The message was clear. Pandavas truthfulness was known to all. Hence, Kaurvas made a strategy to hide Jayadratha.

When next day the battle began, Arjuna became hopeless by the absence of Jayadratha from the battlefield. In the search of enemy Arjuna wasted most of the time of the day. Krishna understood that it was an exercise in futility. Arjuna's search wasn't going to pay any dividend. Lord Krishna employed his magical power. All were hypnotised by the feeling of sunset. A pyre was set for the mighty Arjuna. His brothers and family members gathered there to give him a last farewell. Kaurvas also came their to show their courtesy. They had utmost joy because without Arjuna, the Pandavas wouldn't fight and Kaurvas would be victorious. Jayadratha also reached there to see the demise of Arjuna. When Arjuna was going to enter the pyre all wept but Krishna told him to go there with his weapons. Lord Krishna didn't waste his time in weeping and crying but he was in the process of saving of his friend and disciple Arjuna. When Arjuna stood by the pyre, Jayadratha came near to him. Jayadratha was overwhelmed with joy. In the mean time Krishna disintegrated his magical command over the nature, the sum appeared in the middle of the sky. It was noon. Instantly Lord Krishna ordered Arjuna to kill his enemy. Arjuna took an arrow from his quiver and shot it on Jayadratha. In a single arrow Jayadratha met his end. A new wave of happiness spread in Pandavas camp. This was possible only by the master stroke of Krishna.

A wise manager always keeps some arrows in his quiver to meet unexpected situations. Krishna had always something for risk management. There're hundreds of such examples in his life. Indra became angry and ordered the forces of nature to deluge the entire Brajaboomi (area around Vrindavan). It was Krishna's duty to protect the entire populace of Braja. He brought all people and animals to the foot of Govardhana hill. He dispelled a myth that Indra was the supreme god. If a nation protects its environment and conserves the forces of nature, it will face neither the scarcity of rain, nor flood. He showed his position to Indra. He was a real Management Guru who had measures to meet the natural calamity. Even in modern times advanced and developed nations don't have proper measures to meet natural calamities. Hence, Krishna's life and teachings are inspiring for all ages and nations.

8. Fixed Point Chart and Beyond

या निशा सर्वभूतानां तस्यां जागर्ति संयमी।
यस्यां जाग्रति भूतानि सा निशा पश्यतो मुनेः॥

- गीता

Ya nisha sarva bhootanam tasyam jagarti samyami
Yasyam jagarti bhootani sa nisha pashyato muneh

- From ***'Geeta'***

***Meaning**: When others are in slumber , a conscious person remains watchful. And when all are awaken , a conscious soul takes rest.*

Every economy has certain fundamentals. Every organisation has certain basic points on the basis of which it operates. Every individual has certain traits that reflect his bent of mind. Certain positive points must be maintained. Without such points an economy/organisation/individual will have no existence. One should adhere to one's fundamentals but one shouldn't be a fundamentalist.

We can grow as long as we're receptive. Receptivity makes one learned and skillful. The Ganges is revered as a sacred river in India. It's believed that those who get a drop of the Ganges in the their last moment, become a liberated soul. This is true only on emotional level because we're not talking about the liberation of body but of soul. Hence, we can feel liberation. It's all about feeling. The Ganges is the symbol of purity. By following a path of purity, one can shed the unnecessary weight put on one's psyche. Hence, sipping the holy water of the Ganges in its true spirit one can be a liberated soul. Without imbibing the true spirit one can not understand the fact and move into meditation. Here weight means trifles posed by the society.

The frogs that dwell in the Ganges don't have such spirit. So, they can't be a liberated soul. Imbibing true spirit is possible only for those who've receptivity. Receptivity necessarily demands accommodation of useful and positive ideas disseminated by others. It demands an open ear and open mind.

Fundamentals are one's strength but change is the law of nature. The earth changes her position every moment. The sun also passes through a continuous change. The moon is also the part of this cosmic change. There is only thing eternal in this world. And it is change. We see a flower. We feel its beauty. But the time we take to speak—"It's beautiful." It's no more the same flower. It has changed. If it has been plucked, some portions of it, have been withered within some fragments of a minutes. If it's with the plant, its size, density of its color, its fragrance, its configuration ...... all have gone through many sorts of changes.

Whether we accept change or not, but it's inevitable. Acceptance demands a higher level of mental energy. Normally people remain suspicious towards any new thing/person/idea. But those who're confident, accept. Genuine confidence isn't possible without trust. Here, trust means the trust in entire cosmos. It's not related to any particular religion or way of worship. Trust means trust in truth. Those who don't follow any particular way of worship, may have also trust. Hence, trust hasn't a definite religious connotation. Those who've trust in truth can understand any positive innovation. Therefore, the possibility of acceptance increases in him. He can be confident person. He can assimilate new ideas and employ them for the betterment of his personality and organisation. By this he can strengthen his fundamentals.

An innovative society grows faster. The history of Europe is the history of innovations. There was a time when European nations ruled over this world. Nowadays the U.S.A. is far ahead of European nations in its pursuit of innovation. Hence, it's super power. Some decades ago the erstwhile U.S.S.R. was very much innovative in space research and defense. A Russian cosmonaut was the first person to travel in the space. But the U.S.S.R. couldn't make much innovation in its economic development. Hence, its financial institutions became weak. It has to bring glasnost to upgrade itself but it was a late phenomenon. Its institutions became so much redundant that they couldn't accept the change and hence, the U.S.S.R. was disintegrated into different nations. Nowadays China works vigorously on the basis of other's innovations. It follows other's research and remodel it according to its business demand.

India is an ancient nation. She has a rich culture. She has seen many ups and downs. She has a vast amount of cultural heritage. Her huge bulk of literary scriptures and cultural heritage are the outcome innovative minds. These are the highest specimen of the thinking of argumentative Indians. But From the late medieval times to the early nineteenth century, Indians lost touch with innovations. At most, we can see many decadent trends during that period. Feudal lords were indulged in saving their prestige and luxurious life style. The became the preys of wine and other baser instincts. Court poets instigated their uncontrolled carnal lust. It was only in the nineteenth century, Raja Rammohan Roy pioneered Indian renaissance. He was an innovative mind. He caught the rhythm of fundamentals of India and accepted the best of the west. From here, Indian awakening got its ever soaring height. Buddha became Buddha only because he was ready to go beyond fixed point chart. Karl Marx became Karl Marx because he went beyond the fixed point chart. Here a revolution happened. Krishna was the greatest revolutionary of his time. He was well aware of his tradition and time. His Gita is the reflection of a perfect amalgamation of the traditional wisdom and individual talent. In his time he emerged as the greatest guardian of Indian tradition and the greatest innovator simultaneously.

Lord Krishna had a great respect for elders and learned persons. He was a faithful friend, an obedient son, a dedicated lover, an obedient and intelligent disciple, a great guru and a great revolutionary relevant for all time.

He was ready to change the irrelevant tradition and pioneer a new for the betterment of society. The people of Braj were leading a pastoral life. For such a society preservation of forest is essential. To preserve the forest in the area, it was necessary to preserve the ecological balance of Govardhan (the hilly area of Braja was around the Govardhan mountain range). Hence, Lord Krishna inspired the people to worship Govardhan instead of Indra. His opposition to Indra worship was symbolical. His revolutionary step to worship Govardhan was a great message for preserving our ecological balance.

His marriage with Rukmini was also a pioneering step. Rukmini had heard of the great deeds of Krishna. She had framed an image of Shri Krishna in her mind and had started worshipping him. But her brother (Rukmi) was going to marry her with Shishupal, a wicked person renowned for his notoriety. She sent a message to Krishna to protect her and marry her. When a girl was supposed to be the property of her father/ brother/husband whoever from the male society be in the controlling position in the family. Here question of respecting the feeling of a girl and granting her freedom. If Rukmi would be of the opinion to marry his sister to a good fellow as per the desire of Rukmini, Krishna wouldn't have opposed him. But it was a different case. Rukmi was going to sacrifice his sister for his petty political gain. He had a nexus with all the evil elements of the then Indian subcontinent. To use woman as one's personal property is a crime. Krishna's conscience didn't allow to Rukmi to commit such a heinous crime. He rescued Rukimini against the wishes of her brother Rukmi. He married Rukmini and made his queen.

In the next time the then king of Kamrup had captured sixteen thousand ladies from the different parts of the country. Lord

Krishna defeated the king and rescued all the women. As per the prevalent custom of the time, no one could give shelter to such women. Krishna took a major decision and gave shelter to all of them. All the sixteen thousand ladies resided happily in the Kingdom of Krishna, Dwarka under the patronage of Almighty Lord. This was a revolutionary step in that time. Krishna announced before the Mahabharata war that he wouldn't fight from any side during the war. But once Bhishma started hurling a volley of weapons upon Arjuna and his chariot. For Lord Krishna victory of truth was most important. To achieve this goal, he had to protect Arjuna. Hence, he took a wheel in his hand and rushed towards Bhishma. The grand old man Bhishma was a genuine person. He honoured Krishna and surrendered before him. Krishna became happy very soon and he didn't harm Bhishma. For the betterment of one's organisation one should be ready to change its format as per the demand of time but without moving on a wrong and anti-social track.

9. Team Spirit and Leadership

यस्य देवे परा भक्तिर्यथा देवे तथा गुरौ।
तस्यैव कथिता ह्यार्था: प्रकाशन्ते: महात्मना:॥

– शवेताश्वतर उपनिषद्

Yasya deve para bhaktiryatha deve tatha gurau
Tasyaiv kathita hyartha prakashante mahatmanh

– *From* ***'Shvetashvatar Upanishad'***

Meaining: *Those who have unquestioned devotion in Lord and are guided by their guru with same faith , get a direct realization.*

Lord Krishna was a great guru. He was a great teacher. He was a great leader. He inspired his time and its spirit. His message is relevant for all time. Besides this he was the democratic voice of his time. He articulated people's voice of his time and gave it a concrete shape. The concept of democracy is new and it's a gift of modern age except an example Vaishali Ganrajya (a state of ancient India). But this democracy couldn't come into shape at once. Behind its advent, there has been collective effort of our forefathers. Our thinkers have been stirring people's imagination from the ancient time. There's a great role of argumentative Indians in shaping India as a nation. What we're today, is the collective effort of our forefathers. In this regard, Krishna's voice was a turning point in the history of mankind. The Bhagavadgita is the source of inspiration for millions. The message of Gita was delivered by the Lord in the battle field of Kurukshetra.

Whenever we talk about a democratic voice or collective spirit, going with many and inspiring them, is already inherent in it. Krishna always took care of others. A leader thinks for the welfare of his people. Therefore, he was with people and for people. It's said, at the time of his birth his parents were together in the prison. Chains of his parents and doors of the prison opened automatically at the time of his birth. He came here to free mankind from all kinds of bondages. Since his childhood he was a team man. As a kid he used to play with his friends. He was enjoying the company of milkmen's boys but at the time of need he used to help them. He was himself able to kill Kansa and other monsters but he always took Balrama his elder brother with him. Despite his rare valor he always praised the bravery of Balrama. A true leader inspire his team mates to achieve a goal and appreciate their good deeds. A leader gives true reward to his followers.

A leader should assign any work only to the proper person. After the killing of Kansa, his father-in-law Jarasandha attacked Mathura several times. Jarasandha was doing this only to punish Krishna and the innocent people of Mathura. Krishna understood his intention. To wage a war with Jarasandha would be an exercise in futility. Hence, he shifted his capital to Dwarka. But Jarasansdha must be punished. During a royal sacrifice organised by Yudhishthira, Krishna arranged a dual between Bhima and Jarasandha. He gave Bhima some clues to kill the wicked Jarasandha. He understood hints properly and killed Jarasansdha. Bhima was a proper person for this assignment. A team leader understands the actual capacity of the each member of his team and assign the duty according to one's individual capacity.

At the time of Draupadi's call He himself appeared to save the modesty of a helpless woman. Yudhishthira lost his entire property in the gambling arranged at the behest of Shakuni. What to talk of property, he lost his four brothers and common wife of Panadavas, Draupadi in the gambling. Dushasana at the command of Duryodhana started pulling Draupadi's sari off. In the process he had intention to make her nude. There was no one to help her. In the moment of crisis she prayed Lord Krishna. He came there and supplied sari to her in abundance and safeguarded her modesty. A true leader comes forward in the moment of crisis and helps his team mates.

To eliminate Bhishma form Pandavas way to victory, he took help of Shikhandi. When Shikhandi came between Arjuna and Bhishma, the great warrior Bhishma stopped fighting. In the mean time, Arjuna hurled hundreds of arrows on Bhishma. And Bhishma fell on the ground. A team leader knows that who is fit for a particular task.

He assigned Yudhishthira to speak about the death of Ashvatthama, the only son of guru Dronacharya. And Bhima was assigned to spread this message before Dronacharya. Both of them fulfilled the task adequately. When Dronacharya came to Yudhishthira to verify the news, Yudhishthira said—"Ashvatthama has been killed; either Ashvatthama, the man or Ashvatthama, the elephant." When he said "or the elephant," Lord Krishna blew his conch. In the voice of conch "or the elephant" wasn't heard to Dronacharya. He believed that his son Ashvathama had been killed. In deep sorrow, Drona dropped his weapons. In the mean time, Dhristadyumana came and cut off Drona's head with his sword. A leader assigns work to his team mate but he has to be watchful so that the work could be done properly. Whenever any member lacks the proper direction, he comes to help him. Drona was fighting from the side of unethical forces. Therefore, without eliminating Drona, victory of Pandavas was not possible.

Next big hurdle was Karna. Karna had a lethal weapon to kill his archrival Arjuna. The destructive capability of the weapon was beyond any doubt. He summoned Ghatotkacha to fight from Pandavas side. Ghatotkacha was the son of Bhima from Hidimba. Hidimaba was residing in the forest with his son Ghatotkacha. Ghatotkacha was a mighty warrior and he had knowledge many magical arts. He was able to destroy enemy camp easily. He came into battle field and started hurling magical weapons on enemy forces. No one could stop him. At last Duryodhana requested Karna to use his lethal weapon against Ghatotkacha. He did so to keep his friend happy. With the help of that weapon he killed Ghatotkacha. After this he had no such weapon to fight with Arjuna. When the real battle between Karna and Arjuna took place, Arjuna could kill him. It was the true leadership of Arjuna that led Pandavas to victory. A true leader enjoys the company of his mates, gives them assignment, remains watchful, comes forward in the time of crisis and ultimately lead his team to taste the nectar of victory. Hence, we remember team spirit and inspiring leadership.

10. Vision for Separating Chaffs from Grain

ईश्वरः परमः कृष्णः सच्चिदानन्द विग्रहः।
अनादिरादिगोविन्दः सर्वकारणकारणम्॥

- ब्रह्म संहिता

Eishvarah parmah krishnah sachchidananda vigrah
Anadiradigovindah sarva karankaranam

- *From* ***'Brahma Samhita'***

Meaning: *Krishna is Lord himself. He is the supreme conscience and bliss. There's no beginning and end of the Lord. He is the root of all causes.*

A true management person must have a X-ray vision. He should be able to see different kinds ailments prevalent in his organisation. He should be able to understand the intention of the people with whom he deals with.

A true management guru understands the weakness and strength of his team mates. He must be able to separate chaffs from the grain. Life isn't a bed of roses. It's neither a path full of thorns. No nation or organisation is full of righteous people only. There're good and bad always. A manager should be able to inspire the good in his organisation and eliminate the bad from there. For this he needs a X-ray vision. With the help of his vision he detects whatever the malignant in his organisation. Those who lead an active life has to deal with many sorts of people.

It's not necessary to be involved in fighting with the opponent always. If it's not severe and it'll have no future consequences one should ignore it. If ignoring such a thing will hamper the prospect then one should try to eliminate it.

Lord Krishna had an inborn X-ray vision. When he was a cradle baby, a wicked female monster named Putana came there in the guise of a beautiful lady with an intention to kill the baby Krishna. He felt the wicked touch of the monster. When she started feeding her breast to the baby, he baby began sucking her breast. In the course of sucking the baby took the life of the wicked monster. If the wicked isn't eliminated, it will harm others too. If Krishna hadn't sucked her nipple and destroy her, she might have killed many other babies. If a worthless person isn't shown to the door, he will damage the very fabric of the organisation in the long term. For the health of any organisation a careful manager proceed in this way. During his childhood plays Krishna had to face many problems. But he understood the danger very soon. An expert manager understands the future danger very soon and takes a quick decision to eliminate the danger. In this course he has to safeguard himself always. Without self protection one can't achieve one's goal.

Being gentle isn't enough. You'll have to safeguard your gentleness for personal prosperity as well as community welfare. Many intelligent and skillful persons joins an organisation but he doesn't stay there for a longer spell. Either he relinquishes the organisation or the top management in the organisation compels him to quit. In a few cases such persons leave the organisation for a better career but in most of the cases circumstances force them to take such a step.

If you're intelligent and capable, you should be able to discriminate between friends and foes. There's no mathematical yardstick to separate chaffs from the grain. This is a psychological game. In this mind game one has to proceed cautiously. One shouldn't conclude anything particular in a feat of passion. How to understand has been well discussed in previous chapters.

Krishna understood that Pandavas are good people. They're reliable and the reign of the then India could be handed over to them. He understood that Draupadi could play a positive role in the life of Pandavas. Hence, he promoted her and eliminated the candidature of Karna from her swayamvar. Karna was in the company of wicked persons like Shakuni and Duryodhana. To be the wife of Karna might have diminished her role. She played a major role in the politics and statecraft of her time. She proved herself a genuine strength behind Pandavas. Hence, Krishna's decision was valid.

He helped Draupadi in the moment of crisis. When the news of Rukamini's swayamvar reached him and she requested him to help her. He took a decision and saved her from the trouble. He understood the gravity of the situation. He understood that Rukamini was a beautiful girl and loves him. She was innocent and righteous. Such a beloved must be helped. Her brother Rukami was a wicked person. A wicked must be punished and a good person must be rewarded. Krishna defeated Rukmi in the battle but left him alive because of Rukmini but accepted her hands and married her to be his chief queen. Rukmini was so beautiful that she was compared with goddess Lakshmi. Lord Krishna is said to be the incarnation of Lord Vishnu, the most powerful and handsome god in Hinduism. And Rukmini is said to be the incarnation of Mother goddess Lakshmi. Hence, a natural and eternal love was between them. Krishna renewed the tie.

He was well aware of the wickedness of Shakuni, the maternal uncle of Duryodhana. He was always instigating Duryodhana to wage a war with Pandavas. But Krishna was of the opinion that a war must be a last option. One should initiate dialogue with his enemies. When dialogue doesn't help one should take help of diplomacy. If the diplomacy fails then one should try to strike a deal. If all the options fail and war becomes unavoidable, the one should take weapon to defend oneself. Druapadi had taken a vow that she would wash her hair locks with the blood of Dushasana who had tried to outrage her modesty. Krishna was aware of many such vows. Both the party were ready to fight a mass destructive war. Hence, he tried to strike a deal between them. Against the norm of diplomacy, Duryodhana tried to capture Lord Krishna but he showed his divine might and came out from the court of Dhritrashtra safely. Shakuni had taken a vow to finish the entire Kuru clan because his sister Gandhari had been married to Dhritrashatra, a blind prince of Hastinapura. Father of Shakuni, the king of Gandhara, was not so capable in armed strength to refuse the proposal of Bhishma. After many years of this marriage, at the time of his death he revealed the compulsion before his son Shakuni. He inspired him to took a vow to finish the entire Kuru clan. Krishna was aware of this fact. Hence, he tried to save them. But having found no option, he had a start a war against the nexus of wicked forces. The ultimate war of the time eliminated the wicked from the scene. After that, there was peace in the Indian subcontinent for many centuries.

To separate chaffs from the grain one needs the following qualities:

- A sharp mind
- Wide experience
- Untainted receptivity
- Knowledge of many field
- Hard labour
- Active life
- A charming personality
- A good network
- Friendship from people of different walks of life
- An efficient group of trusted followers
- Promoting the good
- Eliminating the bad

- Setting up a goal for the welfare of the organisation
- Proper direction of emotion
- Master in one's own field
- Confidence in one self
- No fear of taking risk

Lord Krishna had all the above qualities besides being the master of all the divine qualities.

11. Brevity Is the Soul of Wit

उत्क्रामन्तं स्थितं वापि भुंजानं वा गुणान्वितम्।
विमूढा नानुपश्यन्ति पश्यन्ति ज्ञानचक्षुषः॥

- गीता

Utkramantam isthitam vapi bhunjam va gunanvitam
Vimudha nanupashyanti jnanchakshushah

Meaning: *Fools don't understand the changing process of this body and the way this body remains entangled in indulgence. But those whose eyes are illuminated by the knowledge can see everything.*

The English dramatist William Shakespeare said—"Brevity is the soul of wit." When he said this, he wasn't aware of the fact that many thinkers in the world had already employed this fact into their action centuries ago and many will translate this saying into action even in the future. In fact, a poet's imagination catches the gist of centuries. He gives voice to eternal truth.

There are many "ifs and buts" in human life. One has to cross through many zigzags. No success is possible without making one's one path. For this one has to catch the summary of a voluminous text. There is chaos in all walks of life. Some of the problems are imposed by our society and predecessors in different areas. Some of them are due to the individual's own wavering nature. Being concise is a tough task. Here brevity doesn't mean a short-cut path and escape from hard work. Brevity means the acceptance of the essential and the negation of unnecessary things.

Sometimes outspoken nature poses a lot of problems. For this one has to pay a heavy price. Incidentally, when Shishupal was a baby he had four hands (as per the text mentioned in scriptures). This has been said only to express a truth and guide the mankind. It was forecast that his two hands would fall on the earth and he would be a normal child but he would be killed by the person in whose lap the boy would shed his hands. Lord Krishna had a family relationship with Shishupal. He went to Shishupal's house. When he took the boy in his lap, his two hands fell on the ground. His mother requested Krishna that he must not kill her son. Krishna assured her that he'd not kill him till he committed one hundred crimes.

With the passage of time, Shishupal's animosity with Krishna became deeper. He couldn't hide his feelings. He was ready to insult the Almighty Lord at all occasions. Yudhishthira had organised a royal sacrifice after being the king of Indrapratha, a newly founded state. This was an occasion much before the Mahabharata war. In that sacrifice many kings were invited from different parts of the Indian subcontinent. Lord Krishna was prominent among the guests. Shishupal was also invited. The most respected member of Kuru family, Bhishma announced that Lord Krishna would be worshipped first. There was an ages-old tradition of worshipping the most respected guest on such occasions. The Pandavas followed the instruction of Bhishma. All accepted this decision, except Shishupal. He started abusing the Lord. In the beginning, the Lord smiled. He had no habit of speaking unnecessarily. But Shishupal took it otherwise. Krishna warned Shishupal that he would forgive him for his hundred bad words but he'd be punished for crossing that limit. Shishupal didn't stop. He continued to speak abusive words. After one hundred abuses, Lord reminded him of his commitment. But the wicked Shishupal was ready to meet his end. When he spelt one hundred and five such words, Lord Krishna stood up and hurled his Sudarshan chakra (a circular weapon) on Shishupal.

With the mere touch of Sudarshan, Shishupal's head fell on the ground. In the entire process, Krishna maintained his brevity.

The Bhagvadagita is gist of Indian philosophy. In this scripture, the wisdom of the Upanishad has been expressed in a subtle way. One couplet of this book can be explained in a separate book. But the Lord expressed the messages of all the three yoga—Karma (the yoga of action), Bhakti (the yoga of devotion) and Jnana (the yoga of knowledge) in about seven hundred couplets. These shlokas (couplets in Sanskrit) are so beautifully composed that they're sung by a common man also. Arjuna had many questions just before the war. Before realisation human mind questions many things. But after realisation one moves on the path of action. Before realisation Arjuna was seeking an escape from action. But after realisation he proceeded on the path of action more vigorously. Besides making Arjuna a realised person, he provided the hint regarding the outcome of the war. The entire proceeding was done with brevity.

When Draupadi, the daughter of the king of Panchal (modern Punjab) rejected the candidature of Karna in her swayamvar, no one could understand the meaning of the action. Krishna gave her a hint to reject the candidature of Karna without speaking even a single word. When the assembly of kings and princes compelled Panchali to spell out the reason behind her rejection. She gave a befitting answer but some of the members of royal blood weren't willing to be satisfied by her answer and of the intention to give the entire proceedings into another direction. This might have deviated the goal of swayamvar. Lord Krishna took the stage and said—"Whatever may be the reason of rejection but a girl must have the right to select or reject a husband. Depriving a girl from this right would be black day for our country." Lord Krishna's brief statement was a guiding light for coming centuries besides controlling the present situation.

A manager/boss doesn't need to clarify everything and go for lengthy descriptions. People should believe in his integrity.

His men should believe that whatever he decides would be in the betterment of the organisation.

When Dronacharya was posing a problem for the Pandvas during the Mahabharata war and taking unethical means for the victory of Kaurvas, Lord Krishna had to invent only a single sentence for his elimination from the battle field. Dronacharya was part of the team that had slaughtered Abhimanyu (the son of Arjuna). It was a pre decided rule of the war that one brave person will fight with a single person. No person will be surrounded by a group of warriors. A group of warriors surrounded Abhimanyu and killed him mercilessly.

Lord Krishna persuaded Yudhishthira to speak a single sentence. It was—"Ashvatthama has been killed." Ashvatthama, either the man or the elephant (*Ashvatthama hato naro va kunjaroa*). Bhima spread this message in before Dronacharya. This single sentence was enough to eliminate Drona from the battle field. When Yudhishthira spoke the last part (or the elephant) of the sentence, Krishna blew his conch. Drona heard only the killing of Ashvatthama, the man. He was so much depressed by the news that he threw his arms on the ground and sat hopelessly in the battle field. In the meantime, Dhrishtadyumna came there and cut off Drona's head. This was a turning point in the war of Mahabharata. This target could be achieved in a single sentence. Hence, brevity is the soul of wit.

In most of the time Krishna's smile could bring the desired result. What to talk of a sentence. His flute could attract the heart of hundreds of beautiful girls.

Kalyavana was a terror in the entire Indian subcontinent. Once Kalyavana followed him. He chased Krishna to fight a war with him. Krishna ran away. Kalayavana followed him. Krishna entered a cave where a person was in deep meditation. Lord Krishna covered the person with his yellow linen and hided himself at a distant place. Following Krishna Kalayavana entered the same cave. He saw a person sleeping covered in the linen used by Krishna. He believed the Krishna is sleeping and he is tired. He pushed the man in deep slumber by his feet.

The man woke up and saw at him. The man had a boon that the person who make him awake will be burnt into ash. This happened and the wicked Kalayavana was burnt into ash. After the demise of Kalayavana, Lord Krishna came on the spot with a smile and granted the man in sleep with a boon. So without fighting with enemy, he finished him. Hence, brevity is the soul of wit.

But this brevity isn't achieved at once. For this one needs clarity in thought and discipline in action. There must be a co-ordination between thought and action. One needs a clear conscience to take a decision. We find all these things in Krishna's personality.

12. Don't Put Your Feet into Another Indian's Mocassins

स्वभावजेन कौन्तेय निबद्धः स्वनेन कर्मणा।
कर्तुं नेच्छसि यन्मोहात्करिष्यस्यवशोऽपि तत्॥

- गीता

Swabhavjen Kaunteya nibadha svanen Karmana Kartum Nechchhasi yanmohatkarishyasavasho api tat

- *From* **'Geeta'**

Meaning: *For the time being you're under the influence of inertia refusing my instruction but you'll do the same under the compulsion of your own nature.*

Don't put your feet into another Indian's mocassins. This is an old saying prevalent in the North American continent. Here 'Indian' means an aborigine of North American continent. They were the inhabitants found before Christopher Columbus' discovery of the at continent. Moccasin is a type of shoe used by the Red Indians. Putting your feet into another's shoes means leaving no space for the other. Intervening into another's matter isn't expected from you. An uninvited arbitrator is a person who puts his feet into another Indian's mocassins.

Such expression is relevant for all time. One shouldn't deduct any racial reference from such a thing. We often instruct our children—"Mind your business." This can be expressed into a different way. We can say this as "Keep your breath to cool your porridge."

No proverb or idiom is coined on the basis of a single incident. Age old wisdom of mankind find its expression in such a saying. When we look at Lord Krishna's life with a casual look we can say he had interfere into many affairs but with an insightful observation we've another view. The personality of Lord Krishna was so vast and so integral that nothing can be drawn in a haste. His eyes were fixed on the present, his foresight was fixed on the future and his memory had data base related to the past. Many evil elements try to harm him under fear psychosis. Kansa tried to harm him through various monsters on the basis of a forecast. The forecast was—"The eighth son of Devaki and Vasudeva will be an incarnation of Lord Vishnu. He'll kill Kansa." It was enough to disturb Kansa's sleep. He started sending many evil monsters to kill him. Hence, Krishna was forced to be a party in such strives. There was no choice but to fight with such elements. He didn't stand from a side in the Mahabharata war. Duryodhana and Arjuna came to Dwarka to take part in the Mahabharata war. After a formula accepted by the both party, Krishna himself came from Arjuna war to his chariot driver during the war and his entire Yadava army fought from Duryodhana side. Hence, in this war also he didn't put his feet into another's shoes.

In this context we should remember one thing that one shouldn't intervene into another's individual matter but if any matter is going to affect the community life, one shouldn't be indifferent. A matter related to community life is going to have an impact on the individual's life also. An individual is the part of a community. Krishna loved girls of Braja but didn't affect any one's family life. In his presence their life became prosperous. People of Braja loved him with their entire existence. Krishna became their life breath and took care of them. He protected them from all sorts of calamities. He didn't interfere into conjugal life of Pandavas but when none of the Pandavas was able to protect the modesty of Draupadi, he intervened and protected her.

He was well aware with the fact that his parents were imprisoned by Kansa but he didn't go there without the consent of Kansa. He invited Lord Krishna with an intention to kill him. If Lord Krishna had killed Kansa in the beginning he wouldn't be able to kill his other wicked associates. Before a proper invitation from Kansa, he had already killed all the associates of Kansa. After killing Kansa he met his parents.

When Krishna was in the company of Radha, other gopis (girls of Braja) didn't come there. Lalita had same intensity of love for Lord Krishna but she hided her emotion and promoted Radha to go forward. Such a sacrifice is rare in the history of love. She never interfered into Radha-Krishna rendezvous.

Krishna had many queens under the circumstances. During the time of Krishna polygamy of prevalent. It wasn't a crime. But when he was in the company of a queen another queen didn't disturb him. All were following the ethics of non-interference.

Lord Krishna's elder brother Balrama was a sort tempered person. He had a great respect for his elder brother. He enjoyed the company of Balrama. On many occasions he persuaded Balrama to support him. When he supported Subhadhra's kidnapping by Arjuna, Balrama became furious. He pacified Balrama by saying that Subhadra was in deep love with Arjuna. He kidnapped her with the very consent of Subhadra. At same time he make him understand the significance of such a relation. But at another occasion he didn't interfere in the personal decision of Balrama. Before the Mahabharata war both the parties approached Balrama to fight from their respective side. But he refused to fight from any side. Lord Krishna didn't try to persuade him. He honoured his impartiality. On the other hand, Balrama's presence could pose a lot of problems for Krishna. He supported Subhadra's kidnap because it was the question of her happy life. He supported Balrama's decision of not fighting from any side because it was a matter confined to an individual's freedom. Balrama's absence could pave a way to Pandavas victory because Krishna could concentrate on the war and Pandavas' welfare.

Here interference means forceful imposition of one's wishes on another's life. Persuasion for a greater cause for humanity doesn't fall under the category of interference.

When Pandavas accepted the offer of Duryodhana to play gambling, he didn't interfere but when Yudhishthira lost his wife Draupadi in gambling and Kaurvas tried to outrage her modesty he interfered.

Krishna interferes for the welfare of humanity. He interferes to protect the weak. He didn't interfere in Sudama's personal matter but when Sudama sought his help, he helped him whole heartedly. Even after being a wealthy person, Sudama didn't relinquish his habit of exercising self-control. He continued to beg at five houses for his survival. This was a personal decision. He didn't interfere.

When any decision going to affect the health of any organisation, a management person should interfere but he should be silent in a staff's personal matter. When personal relation going to have an adverse impact on the organisation, the person in the helm of affair must intervene. Non-intervention doesn't mean an escape from responsibility. Non-interference is non- imposition of one's personal interest. One's liking and disliking shouldn't be imposed on any person.

This doesn't mean even non-alignment. In this world, non-alignment isn't possible. One has to from a team. But team shouldn't be a gang of conspirators. Lord Krishna formed teams but he broke gangs of conspirators. Jarasandha, Kansa, Shishupal, Kalayavan, Duryodhana and many such persons had gangs of conspirators. They were causing terror for common men. Life had become miserable in the Indian subcontinent. Hence, Lord Krishna came forward to break this nexus.

13. Better Return or Quick Return

सुखदुःखे समे कृत्वा लाभालाभौ जयाजयौ।
ततो युद्धाय युज्यस्व नैवं पापमवाप्स्यसि॥

- गीता

Sukha Dukhe Same Kritva Labhalabhau Jayajayau
Tato yuddhaya yujyasva naivam papamavapyasi

– From **'Geeta'**

Meaning: *Fight a genuine battle without the lustful consideration of victory or defeat and loss or gain. Proceeding through a rightful way with objectivity , you'll have no sin.*

A great soul never performs any task with the hope of any personal gain. He doesn't invests his all skill and resources for the benefit of entire society. His life is for others. His work is selfless in personal context but he works for a return for the society.

There has been discussion on the topic—"Better return or quick return." There's no harm in quick return unless it hampers your long term existence. If there's anything unethical related to quick return it must be discouraged. Besides doing deep into ethics, let me clear it that some investments have the nature of quick return but others may have nature of better return. It depends on the nature of business or product. In the context of Lord Krishna we've a different aspect of return. His works gave a quick relief to the suffering humanity of the time. His life and message are relevant for all time. The Bhagavadgita is an inspiring book for humanity baring caste and creed. He took part in the war of the Mahabharata as a chariot driver. There he played a vital role in leading the Pandavas to victory.

Here Krishna restored truth and values in the society. The victory put an end to the prolonged suffering of the Pandavas. There was a deeper message in Krishna's act. God is the torch bearer for His devotees. He Himself becomes the driver of the vehicle of His devotees. He declares this fact in his Gita sermon – "I take care of all those who worship me with unquestioned devotion." Krishna took care of all the Pandavas. He established the rule of Dharma in the entire Indian subcontinent.

Lord Krishna's place is unique in the history of mankind. He might not have thought in the direction of short term or long term gain for human civilisation. Though according to Hindu scriptures he took birth to eliminate the wicked and to give relief to the innocent. In fact Krishna devoted his life in this direction only. As I've mentioned earlier, he was able to kill Kansa in the very beginning and his parents could be freed. But he didn't proceed in this direction. He was aware of the suffering of his parents. If Kansa could be killed earlier, the problem might not have been solved. Other monsters would have their influence in the other areas. They could pose problems in the other areas. Therefore, Krishna killed Kansa's all associates before killing him. After eradicating the root of problem he met his parents. A great person pushes his person care on the back seat and keeps a greater cause on the front seat of his priority. A manager keeps short term benefit in his mind and focus his attention on the long term gain of the organisation. He doesn't immerse himself into trifles.

Many times for a greater cause he was ready to compromise. He was aware of the vows taken by Bhima and Draupadi but he didn't let personal likes and dislikes block the way to peace. When in the vicious game of gambling Duryodhana had ordered Dushasana to bring Draupadi forcefully in the court and make her seated nude on his thighs, Krishna had protected her modesty. But Bhima took an oath to break to thighs of Duryodhana and drinking the blood of Dushasana by tearing the latter's heart apart. At the same time, Draupadi took an oath to wash her hair with the same blood of Duryodhana and then she would tie her braid. If peace agreement would have taken place between the Pandavas and the Kaurvas, their oaths might not have been fulfilled. Krishna was aware of this aspect but he couldn't stop initiating a dialogue with the Kaurvas to establish peace. Nothing can be given priority at the cost of world peace. Hence, he overlooked Bhima's and Draupadi's respective vows and moved on the path of peace. After the negation of peace process by the Kaurvas, the war of Mahabharata took place. Krishna overlooked short term benefit for the long term gain for humanity. A great leader looks at the main goal of the country/organisation. If short term return is to hamper the very prospect of the organisation, he sacrifices the quick return. If the quick return is possible along with the endeavor for better return it's welcome. But in the hope of better return one shouldn't overlook quick return at once. Sometimes quick return is good for survival. Krishna didn't let other monsters roam freely and killed Kansa at once. He wasn't pursuing the main goal and overlooking minor targets. Most of the times, quick return strengthens the organisation to be ready for better return. Hence, quick return isn't always against better return. Most of the times, they're complementary to each other.

14. Resources Conservation and Exploitation

इहैकस्थं जगत्कृष्णम् पश्याद्य सचराचरम्।
मम देहे गुडाकेश यच्चान्यद्द्रष्टुमिच्छसि॥

– गीता

Ihaikashtham jagakrishnam pashyad sacharacharam Mam dehe Gudakesha yachchanya drashtumichchhasi

– *From* ***'Geeta'***

***Meaning**: O Arjuna, you can observe all living and non-living things in my cosmic form. Besides these you can also observe other things what you wish.*

Lord Krishna's entire life is an ever glittering example of a balance between conservation and exploitation of resources. He made effort to clean water and other resources clean. He became a pioneer in establishing prominent towns of time. But he always kept the welfare of human society at a greater level.

There should be balance between the two. We need plantation but we need wood for constructing buildings. Usually during the last two or three centuries we've exploited our resources but didn't pay our attention towards conservation. Exploitation without conservation leads one towards chaos and destruction. Modern days' consciousness for conservation is a relatively new phenomenon. But in Indian thinking conservation is an essential part. It's ingrained into our way of life. In Durga Shaptasati (A prominent book on the worship of Mother Goddess) it has been said in Kavach hymn— "As long as the earth is full of forest, mountains, garden the future of human generation will be secured and the fertility of the earth will remain intact." Our forefathers were moving in this direction. Even during the rule over India by Arab invaders this thinking was in vogue. It was during the British rule conservation had no place. They exploited resources of India and for this permanent loss the gave India some modern institutions. It was done not as a philanthropic activity but to run their administration. Krishna made his best efforts for the conservation of resources and delivered message in this context for the welfare of entire mankind.

When Lord Krishna was a kid, people of Mathura region were facing a lot of problems. Highly poisonous serpents were residing in the Yamuna. Kalia was most notorious among them. The entire water body of Yamuna was polluted. Animals that drank its water died. Even many men and women of that area also died. Many of them fell ill. These serpent families created terror in the region. In pastoral society river and meadows are the life lines. They must be protected. Krishna heard the news of people's agony. He reached on the bank of Yamuna along with his friends. Boys started playing volley ball. During the game Krishna threw the ball into the river exactly where Kalia and his family members were residing. The boys of opposite team pressed hard to give the ball back. Krishna had no option but to return the ball. He jumped into the river. He fought with Kalia. Accepting Krishna's might Kalia and other serpents left the very place. They fled towards the ocean through the river way. This Indian river is connected to the Ganges. The Ganges meets the Bay of Bengal and this bay is connected to the Indian ocean.

Hence, after this incident, Yamuna became a clean river. Nowadays, the Yamuna is one of the most polluted rivers of India. Industrial pollutants are immersed into it daily. Many sorts of excreta and other wastage are dumped ruthlessly in this water body. Its waters have become poisonous. We should take inspiration from the life of Krishna to clean our rivers. We need an eco-friendly economy. For rains and other benefits from nature people used to worship Indra, a god residing in heavens. Krishna convinced Yadava chieftains of his area to worship Govardhan, the hill range of the Braja area. Preservation of Govardhan was essential for the survival of a pastoral community. Their economy was dependant on the forests, green meadows and hills of the area. Rainfall is also dependant on a balance eco system. He gave a great message to the people of the region. People followed Krishna's suggestion. For this they had to face the fury of Indra. Krishna saved them from onslaught. It left a great message for the coming generation.

Krishna's all acts were related to preserving the nature and wild life. He was a great protector of cows. Cows are important for both pastoral and agricultural communities. He was a great lover of peacocks. Conservation is a great thing. But adopting a jingoist tendency for conservation and creating unnecessary brouhaha isn't a fruitful act. Conservation shouldn't halt the pace of development. Conservation is necessary for human existence. Similarly human beings can't survive without development. When the Pandavas were given Khanadavaprastha (the area of modern Delhi), a barren land, they had no option to build their capital there. If barren tract of land is handed over for development, no one should object it unless the developmental activity becomes hazardous for the locality. The Pandavas founded a beautiful capital in Khandavaprastha. It was named Indraprastha. Before the foundation of Indraprastha was an inhospitable area and this area was full of bushes. Some criminal tribes were residing in the area. They were posing threats to travellers. Hence, it was necessary to reform them. They had cut off all the supply lines from north to south and vice versa. People of the both sides had to travel through different routs. The Pandavas could do so only with the help of Krishna. They burnt some bushes and reformed tribal people to support developmental activities without disturbing tribes' custom, culture and life-style. After clearing the barren land they planted gardens and shadowy trees in the area. Indraprastha became a clean and eco-friendly city.

Conservation is good for human society. But sometimes judicious exploitation of resources in needed for the development. One should exploit the resources judiciously and create new resources enthusiastically. Without exploitation of resources the pace of development will come to a standstill. But too much exploitation leads to chaos and destruction.

Lord Krishna opposed the worship of Indra but suggested the worship of Govardhan in its place. He inspired the Pandavas to burn the bushes of Khandavaprasatha but guided them to built a capital in its place too. Resources needed to be conserved because they're for entire human civilisation. Personal need should be met but personal greed should be discouraged. Lord Krishna discouraged the greed of Kalia but protected the life and property of people living around.

Hence, Lord Krishna's life is a living example of a balance between conservation and exploitation of resources.

Part III

Lord Krishna and Management at Individual Level

15. Love and Romance

आत्मा तु राधिका तस्य तयैव रमणादसौ।
आत्माराम तया प्राज्ञैः प्रोच्यते गूढवेदिभिः।।

– स्कन्दपुराण

Atma tu Radhika tasya tyaiv ramanadasau
Atmaram Taya prajnaih prochyate Gudhvedibhih

– *From* ***'Skandapurana'***

Meaning: *Lord Krishna is God. Radha is His soul. Lord Krishna enjoy the company of Radha. Hence , those who understand this fact call him ' Atmaram'(the eternal lord the soul)***.**

Romanticism was a movement in English poetry. It was started by William Wordsworth and S.T. Coleridge. They jointly wrote the introduction to "Lyrical Ballads." This introduction is known as "Manifesto of Romanticism." In this piece, we find certain features of romanticism.

When common men talk about romanticism, they've no idea of such a literary movement. For common men romanticism has a different meaning. They think that a person who takes interest in love for opposite sex. They've always a heart to love nature and opposite sex. They don't waste their leisure hours in a serious business. The meaning of romance may differ from person to person. Some persons may not be able to conceive the genuine meaning of 'romance' but they've also a perception of this word.

But love is beyond any definition. In Narada Bhakti Sutra (a famous book on the concept of devotion). it has been said— "Love is beyond any description." It can't be described through words (**Anivarchniya Prem Swarupam**). Here we talk about love for God. We don't talk about mundane love, particularly in the context of Bhakti Sutra. Lord Krishna's love was pure. It wasn't carnal because physical love has its limitations. Krishna was in love with millions. When he was in Braja, as a child he had love with each particle of the locale. What to talk of gopis, cattle, flute, music, dance, Madhuban (a garden where Radha and Krishna used to meet) and so on .... He was in deep love with each particle. Such an intense love with the entire locale can't have physical affiliation. It's a matter of heart. It can't be driven by physical lust.

Romance has a superficial level. It has emotional as well as physical drive. But love is beyond any particular cause. Where there's a cause, there's a reason......love can't happen there. Because 'cause' and 'reason' belong to the domain of mind. They're never accepted by heart. If physical attraction or carnal desire pushes one to fall in love, it can't be called love with the person ...... at most it will be a love for the particular cause. Physical beauty is bound to fade with the passage of time. Physical beauty can be medium ...at most. It can't be an end......feeling each other's heart is love. When 'I' is dissolve into lover, it's called Love.

Lord Krishna wasn't an individual in the broader perspective. This personality was so broad ...... so profound that it became the representative of the Supreme soul.

We often talk about Krishna's love for Radha and other girls of Braja but we miss a point at the same time. From different sources of Krishna literature, it's clear that at the age of eleven he left Braja for ever. His love for Radha and others must have before this age. In normal circumstances, a boy of eight or ten years can't understand physical inclination towards opposite sex. Krishna met Radha first time at the age of four or five. They fall in love with each other in the first sight. We can't think of any romance of physical love at that age.

Krishna had left Braja and settled in Mathura at the age of twelve. He had feeling that Gopis would be suffering due to separation from him. He sent his friend Uddhava to make gopis understand. Uddhava went there and try to persuade gopis to resume their normal life. He tried his best to convince gopis to lead a normal life and forget Krishna because life is short and time is fleeting. There's no benefit to suffer in the separation of Krishna. This body will perish one day. He told gopis to concentrate on formless God. Gopis smiled at the childish method of Uddhava. They retorted—"We do not have many hearts, we had only one heart and it went away, with Lord Krishna. There's no scope for others here." This is called love.

There's one critical episode in the life of Krishna. And it's open to interpretation. This is the theft of dress of Gopis taking bath in the river. During ancient time the society was more open and liberal in India. Women didn't use to put veil on their head. This system came in India after Islamic invasion. Invaders started outraging modesty of beautiful ladies. To save themselves, Hindu women started putting veil. It is the same as the burqa put on by Muslim ladies. In ancient India, ladies used to take bath in completely nude position, though in a secluded position. There were no bathrooms of modern style. Male members of the society were bound to regard them. There may be a different reason. During the time weaving wasn't a wide spread profession. It was on a limited scale. There were no textile mills. To wear the same dress on two or three days, women didn't wash their dresses daily. They had kept them on the bank of the river and then they used to swim in the river.

But during Krishna's time society was going through a transitional phase. Wicked monsters were roaming in towns, villages and hinterlands. Therefore, it was necessary to convince ladies to abandon such practices. One day some Gopis were taking bath in a seclude place in Yamuna. On that bank there were many shadowy trees provide soothing comfort. Mild breeze touching their leaves used to provide solace to the tired ladies of the locality. They were very simple and innocent girls of Krishna's age. When they were deeply engaged in water game and swimming, Krishna came their and took their dresses silently. After sometime they looked towards their dresses but couldn't found. In the moment of crisis they used to remember their Krishna. Krishna appeared before them. They covered their bodies up to shoulders in the water.

They requested Krishna to give back their dresses. After much request Krishna returned their dresses but with an assurance to discontinue this practice of naked bath. They assured him. The girls were of same age group. A boy may be naughty. Here may be an element of romance in the episode. Spiritual leaders give a very sublime connotation of this episode. They say— "Lord Krishna is a Supreme Soul. He wanted to destroy all sorts of hesitation from their devotees mind. In the eyes of God, there's no distinction between a male and a female. Divine world is above gender discrimination."

Krishna was a living example of eternal love. He promoted love. He himself married to the girls who were in intense love with him. He married eight girls after achieving an age. Polygamy was prevalent in that time. It wasn't considered as a crime. Krishna married to different ladies under different circumstances and with the consent of the women already married with him. He gave patronage to sixteen thousand ladies freed from jails. All of them led a dignified life under his patronage. He had no physical relation with any one of them. Love needs a dedication. Love demands purity of heart. A genuine person loves; don't promote romantic and lecherous tendencies. If romanticism is confined to a taste for beautiful things and nature, then there is nothing wrong in being romantic. But if romantic tendencies are the hunger for physical lust, then it must be discouraged. Krishna discouraged Duryodhana's effort to insult the woman's body (in the case of Druapadi). Hence, Krishna was a symbol of pure love. His love was above the demarcation between platonic and carnal. His love was eternal, full of respect and trust in the entire existence.

16. You've Got Only One Chance

सर्व गुह्यतमं भूयः शृणु मे परमं वचः।
इष्टोऽसि मे दृढ़मिति ततो वक्ष्यामि ते हितम्॥

- गीता

Sarva Guhyatamam bhooyah shrinu me paramam Vachah
Ishtoasi me dridh miti tato Vakshyami te hitam

– *From* ***'Geeta'***

Meaning: *You are very dear to me , so I tell you the supreme and sacred knowledge of mine. Listen to me for your own welfare.*

You're not going to find another chance. This is one of the prime motivational statements to push one to strive hard to achieve one's goal. In fact human life is very short. But in this short life we've examples of many great persons who achieve extraordinary things in their life. It depends on the way you look at life and utilise your resources and time. Utilisation of what you've is a great management skill. If anyone utilises what he has, he can achieve the thing that looks impossible. You can get what you don't have from the thing what you have.

Jesus had a vision to give. He showed the way and reached the place that is far from the maddening crowd. Gandhi had determination, integrity, non-violence and a vision to make

India a free nation. He did so with utmost dedication. And India became an independent nation. He's called father of the nation. Buddha was an ordinary prince of a small kingdom but by his effort he became a torch bearer for millions. From Siddhartha to Buddha, there was a flow to fulfill one's inner. To understand the—"why there's sorrow in human life?"

Those, who say—"I'll do it tomorrow," never reach their destination. Destiny doesn't favour them. Those who say- "I'll do it" and don't take rest before doing it, taste the fruit of success.

Life is very precious. You've got only one chance. Here chance isn't confined to achieving success only. We've get many things. Pleasure and rest can't be overlooked. Without a sustainable level of pleasure, life has no meaning. Hence, we've to labour hard for achieving success and design of our life style so that we would be able to enjoy a healthy life.

In this life we need sensitivity to understand ourselves and others. You need to feel your pain and pleasure and those of others' too. One should try to distribute pleasure and destroy pain of all. An individual must have a community life. This isn't a part of research thesis or philosophical treatise or speculation. This is relevant to enjoy a life full pleasure.

A Simple Mantra

To lead a life full of pleasure

We need to grow

We grow when we share

We grow when we care

We grow when we dare

This happens everywhere

When we're aware.

When we live with an awareness to utilise what we've we start growing. This awareness makes one responsible. I don't encourage you to be serious. That's because seriousness spoils our sense of humour. I want to use dedication in the place of seriousness. A suggest responsible effort instead of an exercise in futility. Those who employed this idea touch the zenith in their life.

Krishna performed his all tasks with utmost dedication. He had to fulfill all his responsibility in that life only. On the one hand he had a band of dedicated friends and on the other hand he had to face a gang of wicked persons. In the life you can't overlook any one of them. You can't escape from the harsh reality and problems of life. But ignoring the beauty of the world will make the life meaningless.

A boy is born. But lives only for 3 years. This seems queer. But when you focus your eyes on the business of life, you'll be able to comprehend the meaning of this sentence. After three years, he goes to school. Schools aren't for giving you a life you're meant for. They're in competitive atmosphere. A child had to bear the pangs of the competition. In the school, all efforts are made to turn one into competitive device. After this phase he becomes a responsible citizen and carries the baggage of his family and career. Besides this he becomes the victim of his own whims and fancies. Where is that life for which we've lost this life?

Hence, you've got only one chance means you'll have to manage everything in this life. Ignoring isn't a management. Management is solution and growth. Lord Krishna never ignored any problem. He never ignored any one's love. He any overlooked any tears. He never allowed any wicked to roam freely. In midst of all these things he used to play flute. He used to dance with the girls of Braja. He often combed his beautiful queens.

When Kansa invited him in Mathura, he was aware with the fact that a fight between them would take place but he didn't ignore Kubja. Kubja was a maid in the court of Kansa. Her duty was to provide sandal paste in the palace. She was a hunched back lady. For her physical deformity, she wasn't receiving an affectionate eye from any corner. She had a great love and respect for Lord Krishna. Her only desire was to apply sandal paste on the forehead of the Lord. Krishna understood her desire. He approached to Kubja. He touched her hunch with a delicacy. She became so much elated by the intimate touch of the Lord that within some minutes her deformity was cured and she became a beautiful lady. Krishna accepted her sandal paste.

Real success is to get it along with others. If we help others to enjoy a meaningful life, then our life is really meaningful. Ignoring any one of our responsibility won't allow us to be happy. We're responsible for our children, spouse, parents, elders, community, nation and this world. Life is so integrated that a rose petal is plucked in India, the land of distant poles shakes. Though its intensity isn't visible but it has its impact.

Lord Krishna was a cute baby, a dedicated lover, an obedient son, a disciplined student, a mighty warrior, a great guru, a responsible husband, a faithful friend, a genuine reformer, a true revolutionary, a handsome superman, a great father and above all the Supreme soul. His love had so much intensity and depth that when after a gap of many decades he met Radha at Kurukshatra, other ladies in the company of Radha asked her—"Whether Krishna is same or he is a changed man?" She responded without any delay—"Though his body has grown but he's the same Krishna. He's my Krishna even now...Radha's Krishna." In the entire region of Kurukshetra, " Radha-Krishna, Radha-Krishna ..." echoed.

He fought monsters with the same intensity. He went to Guru Sandipani's school and studied there with the same dedication. He guided Arjuna and the Pandvas in the war of the Mahabharata with the same skill and experience. His dedication, his nature, his labour ...all such qualities made him a house hold name in India.

Life becomes meaningful with dedication. It becomes inspiring with integrity. It becomes divine with righteousness. It celebrates success with conscious labour. It becomes a festival with awareness. And it's possible when we believe that we've got only one chance.

Let the life become a celebration. Let the life become a festival, just like our Lord Krishna did and we can also do.

17. Balance between Two Worlds

अन्यायश्चिन्तयन्तो मां ये जनाः पर्युपासते ।
तेषां नित्यभियुक्तानां योगक्षेमं वहाम्यहम्॥

- गीता

Ananyanshachintayanto mam ye janah paryupaste Tesham nityayuktanam yogakshemam vahamyaham

*- From **'Geeta'***

***Meaning**: Those who regularly meditate with utmost devotion upon my divine form get fulfilled all their worldly and spiritual needs.*

A surrealist says—"There's no pleasure in life. It's full of pain and misery. There's no love in life. There is an artificial drama in the name of love. Life is full of thorns. No flower blooms in life. There's hunger and chaos in our life. It is meaningless." This sort of hopelessness and dejection are the outcome pessimistic ideologies.

This sort of ideologies immerge when the community suffers from a prolong strife and misery. And an author has to write on belly.

Life is divine but for only those who've got chance and put their effort to make it comfortable.

Life isn't unidirectional. One has to take care of his both

worlds—outer and inner. We have our outer world every moment. Our existence is in this world. But without our inner world we've no existence. Life has meaning even for those who continuously say—"it's meaningless." A surrealist has felt the dark side of life. Without inner world no one can feel. No one can feel that there're thorns only. No one can feel that there's chaos. No one can feel pangs of children die due to hunger in Sahara. But at the same time without inner no one can feel the beauty of the Taj. No one can feel the beauty of a girl ...without inner no one can feel the breath of his beloved. Without inner no one can feel the beauty of a snow clad peak, no one can feel dancing waves on the beaches.

We see our outer world but we feel through our inner. Inner isn't only a medium to peep the world through. It's the existence. It is our inner that makes us human beings. Without inner we're a mechanical accumulation of flesh and bones.

We can't ignore any one. We'll have to take care of the both. Fighting with wicked monsters and cruel kings was the demand of the outer world of Krishna but to play with his boyhood friends was the quest of the inner. Dancing with girls was the demand of his inner. Running away from Mother Yashoda was the part of his childhood divine acts. It was for pure pleasure.

One has to follow diurnal demands but ignoring pure pleasure for the sake of material prosperity is to waste life for trifles. One shouldn't be lost into trifles.

Krishna took care of his both worlds. He founded Dwarka at the sea coast of Gujarat. Under his leadership it became one of the most prosperous kingdoms of India. But while discharging his royal responsibilities he never forgot to play his flute. Even during the Mahabharata war he used to keep his flute with himself. It's said—he was so fond of his flute that he didn't allow even Radha to touch it, although he used to play it for Radha.

Arjuna was a great warrior but Krishna inspired him to seek divine blessings before the war. Earlier Arjuna had performed penance to please Lord Shiva. Lord Shiva blessed him and gave him Pashupatashtra (a mighty weapon for killing enemies). Before the Mahabharata, Krishna advised Arjuna to go to the Trikuta mountain peak in Jammu region to seek the blessings of Mother Goddess, Vaishno Devi. And he followed the advice.

To get success, one needs his personal effort, guru's guidance, elder's affection and divine blessings. We've instances of success achieved by some atheists but they lead a life in opposition. They're under the impact of his labour. He misses many things. Divine blessings have a soothing effect on one's mind. If we lead a spiritual life, we feel peace and pleasure. Here seeking divine blessings doesn't mean unnecessarily wandering for seeking helps from quacks and so called spiritual persons. There're many magicians roaming in the guise of saints. Beware of them. Krishna's advice was—seek divine intervention without ignoring one's own duty. In his Gita lecture he advocated for the yoga of action. But along with this went into the detail of the other yoga—yoga of knowledge and yoga of devotion. The latter two types of yoga are related to our inner. We've to translate our inner thought into action. This is the gist of yoga of action.

There must be a balance between one's spiritual and material worlds. The society that ignores its material world is destroyed by a violent civilisation. A civilisation without spiritualism becomes chaotic. Hence, there must be an order in life. Arjuna had faith in his own might and trust in Lord Krishna's blessings. When he was offered to choose either Krishna or his Yadava warriors, He opted for the former. Spiritualism brings a rhythm in our action. Such action becomes fruitful for entire mankind. When we look at the great surviving civilisations of the world, we find that they gave proper attention to their both worlds. A balanced life never pushes any one towards any anarchy. A balance life makes one life musical. In his childhood Lord Krishna used to bring his cows for grazing in meadows. When they started grazing, Krishna used to play his flute. Cow grazing was an essential aspect for pastoral community but playing flute was for pleasure.

Here, we find a mind-body synergy. At his last moment, a hunter shot an arrow at him by mistake but he smiled and forgave him. He led an eventful life but there was always smile on his lips. Hence, he lived a balance life ....a blissful life. I salute this extraordinary life.

18. God Is Ready to Bless You

कर्मण्येवाधिकारस्ते मा फलेषु कदाचन।
मा कर्मफलहेतुर्भूमा ते संगोऽस्त्वकर्मणि॥

\- गीता

KarmanyeVadhikaraste ma phaleshu kadachan
Ma karmaphalheturbhooma te sango astvakarmani

From ' **Geeta**'

Meaning: *You've right to perform your duty but the result isn't under your complete command. Don't blame yourself fro any result and don't be entangled into a lustful attachment with it.*

We often hear a statement—"My fate doesn't favour me." We've many versions of this statement—Nowadays my constellation isn't in a good position, My misfortune is the result of my previous sins, I'm in the worst phase of my life, My destination is against my will and so on....

All these statements are perceptions based on the present happenings. But divine source isn't confined to the present happenings. It takes care of the past, the present and the future. Our present position depends on many factors—our thought, our action, and our surroundings. No doubt surroundings and bringing up have a great role in shaping an individual's destiny. But one can excess in life with or without this. It depends on one's determination and effort to pursue goal. God is ready to bless a determined person.

Some persons have to work in mines and factories just from the beginning. They don't get opportunity to enjoy their childhood. But even some persons from this lot pursue to achieve a goal and become successful. A child from an economically backward area has to struggle much to achieve even a petty thing in his life. Hence, ambience has a great role, destiny has a greater role and individual has the greatest role in shaping one's own life.

The statement in the title is based on the message delivered by Lord Krishna in his Gita. He said "Concentrate on action. Don't be anxious for the result." In the first glance this statement seems peculiar but it has a greater significance when we think it at a deeper level. In an organisation or at an individual level we fix a goal and work accordingly. Fixing a goal is necessary from motivation aspect. Without any expectation or motivation we won't be able to perform. Hence, fixing a goal is the begging of life in expectation. If we're in expectation, it may affect our concentration to perform duty. Here we need management skill. And Lord Krishna has indicated us to be equipped with such a management skill. Concentration on action means employing our maximum potential to our work. If an action is done with hundred percent dedication, the result will be achieved. Here, concentration doesn't mean hundred percent physical involvement. It's a mind game. In this game one has to employ one's mind, body and soul—all together. Oxen and asses labour with their body, they're driven by others. Horses run fast but they are controlled by their riders. An intelligent manager works by his intelligence, instinct, body, mind and soul. All are employed to bring a rhythm in his action. Only after employment of our all skills and body-mind-soul we can achieve a great thing. In the battle field of the Mahabharata, Krishna gave this message to his friend and disciple Arjuna. He advised him to concentrate on his action.

This message can be understood only by those who've a wider experience in their life. There're many elements in our life that create wavering. These elements affect our action. To concentrate on our action, Lord Krishna advised Arjuna to overcome the duality of pain and pleasure. Is it possible?

Without pain or pleasure, what is life? Right, there is pleasure in our life and there're moments of sorrow too.

Without duality of pain and pleasure, sorrow and happiness etc. life isn't possible. But to remain attached to such duality one's mental balance is affected. Before the war of the Mahabharata, Arjuna became sentimental. He saw his kiths and kin ready to fight from both sides. He confined the war at his personal level. But for Krishna, it was fight between the good and the evil. Krishna's main concern was—the establishment of a righteous social order. When Arjuna requested him to position his chariot between the two armies, Krishna did so. He clarified Arjuna's doubt and made it clear that it was a fight between constructive and destructive forces. In such a war one should fight from constructive side.

Escaping isn't the answer. You can't escape from life. In a decisive battle one will have to participate. Avoiding a tough situation doesn't make life easy. On the other hand, it makes life critical, more complex. Life demands decision and action accordingly. Arjuna was trying to avoid a tough situation for saving the life of his close relatives. In our daily life, we see people committing many crimes to save their corrupt relatives. In Bollywood films, we watch a villain father saving his corrupt sons. For this he commits many crimes. In the process many innocent people are killed. At last a hero comes to save the masses from the barbarism of the villain. In the end justice is done. This is in reel life but we face such a situation in our daily life.

Indifference of masses to any serious issue brings many types of imbalances in the society. In such an ambiguous situation, it becomes difficult to discriminate between right and wrong. Scenario looks fluid. It brings chaos. Hence, it's the duty of every individual to raise his voice for the sake of truth. One should be responsible member of society. Only a responsible person can be useful to his organisation. An escapist has no worth. It's a better to accept death than leading a worthless life. Krishna had the complete knowledge of Arjuna's worth. He didn't allow his fellow to talk like a worthless person.

Therefore, he delivered his sermon. The message of the Bhagavadgita is universal. It's perfect amalgamation of philosophy and psychology of human life. People often leave everything to God. No doubt, there is God. He helps people. He blesses a genuine person. All religions say this fact. But in the name of God one shouldn't avoid burning issue. Life is so integrated, so meaningful that if we pluck a flower in India, the land of the U.S.A. shakes, although it's on such a minute scale that people don't feel it. But it's a fact. Each action has a reaction. Thus avoidance isn't a solution.

Krishna was aware that Arjuna's escape from the war had a wrong impact on Duryodhana and wicked persons. They would have concluded that Pandavas were cowards. They would have started harassing people more vigorously. Hence, it would have led more chaos, more anarchy.

An individual's action is not confined to his life only. He is related to a family, a society, an organisation etc. Activity of each member is related to the growth of a society. That's why a well designed organisation doesn't tolerate an escapist. How could Krishna tolerate Arjuna's escapism? Through Krishna—Arjuna dialogue mankind got a universal message.

One should be kind and helping but one shouldn't be swayed by wrong affiliations. In the name of relationship, one shouldn't promote wrong practice. An organisation looses it's brightness due to wrong practices. Once a question mark is put on credibility, the death of an organisation begins. Arjuna understood a deeper meaning of life. He had all the qualities of a successful person but he needed a deeper understanding. To play if all walks of life, one needs a deeper understanding.

Krishna understood in the midst of battlefield along with Arjuna. It has also a deeper significance. Krishna was the Lord of Yoga and Arjuna was a student of yoga. They were in the midst of the battle field. Life is battle. We've to face the duality in life every moment. Those who stand unmoved by dualities and work in a righteous way are to be called the Lords of yoga. A tough guy isn't move by a situation but he put his endeavor to move the situation. Arjuna became moved by the situation but Krishna removed Arjuna's sentimental hang ups.

Those who believe in yoga of action don't escape from a situation. They face it, whatever the result may be. If one the very beginning of the foundation of an organisation, one starts thinking of making it number one in its respective field it will have no harm. But if he has any doubt in the mind regarding success, his action will be adversely affected. One should start his work with full care and confidence. Even a smaller success is significant. We compare ourselves with others and be little our effort. One should be watchful, one must have comparative and analytical brain but without hundred percent efforts desired success isn't possible. To get such a success one has to labour hard. There's no alternative to action. After doing a completely dedicated action, one gets success. Krishna inspires Arjuna to perform such an action. After this sort of action God is ready to bless you. To be lazy in the name of God won't bring any result.

19. Presentation Skill

बुद्धियुक्तो जहातीह उभे सुकृतदुष्कृते।
तस्माद्योगयाय युज्यस्व योगः कर्मसु कौशलम्॥

- गीता

Budhiyukto jahateeha ubhe sukritadushkrite
Tasmadyogayay yujyasva yogah karmasu Kaushalam

– *From* ***'Geeta'***

Meaning: *Those who are engrossed in the yoga of devotion, get detached from the duality of action. To acquire this skill is the supreme endeavor in the life.*

Content is important but packaging is equally important. Sometimes, a girl having ordinary looks is crowned Miss World. Another girl of same look doesn't taste the glamour that touches the feet of beauty queen. One has worth, one has skill, one has a beautiful look, one has a clean heart and so on ......but he never gets success. He follows success but never catches it. Success remains a mythical swan for him. He is unable to pat the shining wings of the swan. He never sees even an oasis in the desert of his life, what to talk of seeing an actual water body and quenching thirst!

Here comes presentation. Without presentation skill one can't make a point. In an examination a student present his answer. But those who've a better presentation skill get higher marks. A trainer presents his knowledge and experience. By this way he trains his trainee. A successful person has a great presentation skill.

Let me clear one thing that a genuine presentation is possible only through a genuine way. One can make fool of a person for sometime but one can't always make a fool of that person. To have a sustainable presentation skill one needs genuine qualities.

Krishna's life was full of divine qualities. His each word was meaningful. He led a meaningful life. Everyone praised his divine qualities. Even his enemies were influenced by his qualities. As we've already discussed that before the war of the Mahabharata, Arjuna had some queries. To disperse the cloud of doubt from his mind Krishna presented the meaning and goal of life in such a way that a dejected Arjuna took weapons in his hands and came forward to fight with evils.

His charming attitude attracted people to his side. The girls of Braja were in love with Krishna in (an expressed or unexpressed manner). For presentation on should have knowledge of place and person with a proper sense of timing. Krishna had a different attitude towards gopis and his attitude changed with warriors of the time. He was always an innocent child for his mother Yashoda. He was always a loving boy for his Radha. He was the dutiful husband in the eyes of his queen. He was a savior brother in the eyes of Draupadi. He was a wanted enemy for Kansa. He spent his life under the shadow of death at Krishna's hands. Krishna could manage these entirely different roles because his presentation skill was perfect.

In the beginning of the Mahabharata war he delivered Gita lecture. Arjuna was convinced but not by simple logic. Gita dialogue has been divided into eighteen chapters. Each chapter deals with a different topic. In the first chapter, we find the description of Arjuna's sentimental and dejected mind-set. In the second chapter, there's a description of immortality of soul. In the third chapter, there's yoga of action. In the fourth chapter, there's description of knowledge, devotion and action yoga. In the fifth chapter, we find a description of action and renunciation and the relationship between these two. In the sixth chapter, there's description of yoga of self control. In the seventh, we have the yoga of knowledge and science. In the eighth, there's description of Supreme Soul, the eternal. In the ninth chapter, there's a focus on the yoga of divine knowledge and the mysticism of life. In the tenth chapter, we find a description of manifestation of God, the almighty in best things of the world. What is supreme is God. In the eleventh chapter Arjuna saw the cosmic form of Lord Krishna. In the twelfth chapter, there's yoga of devotion. In the same manner next chapters deal with different but related topics. In the last chapter he announces that he is convinced, there's no doubt in his find. In the Gita we find a psychological deal up to a great extent. Up to tenth chapter Krishna tried to convince Arjuna as a friend on different related topics but he is not convinced. When Krishna presented his cosmic form, Arjuna surrendered before him. There was no scope of questioning after the eleventh chapter. After this chapter the tone of Gita changed. Here Krishna became a guru and Arjuna a disciple. Here Arjuna behaves like an enlightened person. To convince any one first one has to behave in a friendly manner. But to be in a friendly position isn't enough. To convince any person, one needs reality. Krishna was talking about life and death before the tenth chapter. He dealt with different branches of knowledge. He delivered a point in favour of yoga of action. Arjuna was paying heed to his lecture but his question was making it clear that he was not convinced. In the tenth chapter, the Lord declared that whatever best you find on the earth is the manifestation God. Here he declared himself God. Despite declaring himself God he couldn't convince Arjuna. At last he appeared in his cosmic form. Arjuna saw the reality. Here, he understood the meaning of the last ten chapters. One needs a demo to prove the worth and utility of his product. Words should match the reality to convince any one.

Observation of reality depends on one's perception. Perception is the sum total of many tendencies. Krishna gave Arjuna a divine vision. Now Arjuna became equipped with a better vision. He foresaw the death of Bhishma, Duryodhana and many warriors from opposite side but he didn't foresee the death of his son Abhimanyu. What's reason? We know that Arjuna's son (Abhimanyu) was killed in the war of Mahabharata. He was expecting the death of warriors from his enemy side but couldn't expect any death from his side. His expectation influenced his perception. He couldn't see the entire reality presented by Lord Krishna. He saw as per his expectation and got convinced. People have expectation and they want to see the world as per their expectations. People seek gurus and savior. When they find such a suitable person, they're convinced. Girls frame a picture of their ideal partners in their mind and boys make an imaginary picture of their future partner. When they get such a picture in flesh and blood in their real life, their life starts becoming pleasant and convincing. But when they don't find such a picture in their real life and what they get are contrary to their mental landscape, their life becomes miserable. In most of the cases people don't get their expectation translated into reality. Hence, most of the marriages have a tragic end.

If anything is presented as per expectation it becomes convincing. Krishna was an omniscient personality. He was aware of one's past, present and future. His action wasn't confined to one's present welfare. A salesman concentrates on the present deal. A visionary takes care of future but God takes care of all time. Krishna didn't put his endeavor to convince Arjuna in a salesman style. His style was unique. He had utmost welfare of mankind in his mind.

For a better presentation one needs a better and deeper understanding of the past, present and future. He said to Arjuna—"I told the sun God in the beginning of the world what I'm talking with you now." This sentence is enough to describe his age old experience.

Short term approach may be convincing but it doesn't work. We talk about sustainable development. We expect a development that is in tune to meet the expectation of future generation. A trainer puts his effort to make trainee more skillful. Training is imparted to make the trainee an asset to the organisation. The individual may not stay in the organisation, he may be a job hopper but his training will be an asset to the particular industry. A skillful person is not only an individual beneficiary but he's an asset to the society. Society grows with the growth of individual.

Krishna presented the case of Pandavas in an excellent manner before Indian masses and members of royal families. Hence, public opinion was against the Kaurvas. Half the battle was won before the actual war. All senior fighters from Kaurvas side were dejected before the war. They were convinced that they were fighting from wrong side. Their heart was from Pandvas side. With the help of dejected soldiers one can't win a war. To win a war one needs a group of enthusiastic and motivated persons.

Without presentation skill, an individual has to live a life in seclusion or to go with the wrong side. Karna was a great warrior but he has no presentation skill. He couldn't present his case properly. He went with the wrong side and ultimately he had to loose the battle of life. Nowadays, some persons due to their dishonesty belong to wrong side. But many fellows have no presentation skill and they aren't in a position where they should have. Lord presented all his action and deeds in an excellent manner. He presented his message in an excellent manner. Hence, the Gita is relevant even today. Lord Krishna is relevant for all time. His life and message will be helpful for all those who want to excel in their life—either in spiritual or in worldly life or in the both.

20. Overcoming Hesitations and Inhibitions

नष्टो मोहः स्मृतिर्लब्धा त्वत्प्रसादान्मयाच्युत।
स्थितोऽस्मि गतसंदेहः करिष्ये वचनं तव॥

– गीता

Nashto Mohah Smritirlabdha tvatprasadan mayachyutah
Ishthito asmi Gatasandeha karishye Vachanam tava

– *From* **'Geeta'**

Meaning: *O eternal Krishna you have dispelled my illusion. By your grace I have regained my mental power. Now I'm free from doubt. In this stage of determination I'm ready to follow your instruction.*

There're many sorts of hesitations and inhibitions in our life. Hesitation stops us to say what we want to say. Inhibitions are related to our past experiences. Krishna's personality was beyond any hesitations and inhibitions. He put forward what he considered truthful and valid.

Pandavas were suffering from hesitations from the beginning. On the other hand Duryodhana was suffering from shameless audacity. He was under the influence of sinful elements represented by his maternal uncle Shakuni. Dhritrashtra was suffering from inhibitions. He was an indecisive person. He was seeking his benefit in his indecisiveness. Krishna was never in indecisiveness. He was a living example of divinity incarnate. Being indecisive from his part would mean anarchy in life and society.

Krishna decided to kill Putana, an ogress. He did kill her when she came to feed him poisonous milk. Putana came there in the guise of a mother but with an intention to kill the baby Krishna. A mother is mother. To blame the name of a mother is a shameful act. The culprit must be punished. No hesitation. Lord Krishna killed her.

Lord Krishna decided to worship Govardhana, the representative of nature and the locale. Future of mankind is dependent on the conservation of nature. Conserving our resources makes us resourceful. He decided once and tried to convince the persons who were at the helm of affair. He had a unique style. Once he decided, he proceeded to follow the target. Some elders had inhibitions. They were following a wrong notion that Indra was the god of nature and rainfall. But Krishna's attitude was scientific. He was convinced that rainfall is the result of ecological balance. He pursued his ideals and achieved the result. Even now a days many people are influenced by the wrong notions what affected the then elders. But Krishna with his communication skill persuaded them, convinced them and inspired them to move in a proper direction. When Indra tried to destroy the entire Braja land to take revenge, Krishna stood for the people and defeated Indra. This incident dispersed the cloud of hesitations and inhibitions from the mind of elders. They used to believe that what Krishna decided was true. Past experiences give shape to our hesitations and inhibitions. Those who've been brought up under a suppressed ambience, lead a life in hesitations and inhibitions. Those who've spent their childhood in a free and thoughtful ambience, live a mirthful life where there's no scope of hesitations and inhibitions.

Most of people live under a certain impression. We've a certain feeling for a community and a nation. We act accordingly. In recent years, some members of a certain community indulged into some fundamental activities. On the basis of this data, some people conclude that the particular community is the community of terrorists. It's a logical fallacy. No conclusive remarks can be issued of the basis of such a wrong notion.

Similarly we've certain impressions of opposite sex. We behave with them keeping that impression in our mind. Hence, we live a virtual life. To lead an actual life, we need to understand the person, not personality. Personality is an aggregation of inner self and outer presence. But the person is beyond the personality. Personality has certain traits but it is a changing conception. We meet a person after ten or twenty years we find him a changed personality but when we into the deeper layer we find the person is the same whom we had seen a decade or two ago.

We don't deal with a person. We deal with a personality. Krishna played the game at both levels. He dealt with persons and personality. As personality he had a different impression on ordinary people. Gopis understood his person and personality, both. They liked Krishna's attire, style, smile and action but at the same time they understood, Krishna the person……Krishna the supreme soul. Lord Krishna left Braja before the beginning of his teen age but left a permanent impression on the people of Braja. Some months after his departure from Braja, his messenger (Uddhava) came to Braja to give solace to the wounds of gopis that were inflicted on their hearts by their separation from their lover, Krishna, affectionate Krishna, charming Krishna, darling Krishna, Lord Krishna, savior Krishna, God Krishna and so on.... Uddhava tried to convince them to forget Krishna. They could forget him if they would have loved him for his outer presence. They went deeper into the personality of Krishna and discovered the person Krishna. In most of the cases of so called love, result is failure because people love personalities, they don't love the person. No doubt personality is a medium to go into a person. Person is pure but personality is an impression. Lovers come closer to personalities but stay their only with persons. Meeting of personalities is a temporary happening but meeting of persons is a permanent tie up.

One question—who has the time to discover personality? Answer is very simple. Seeker of peace and genuine prosperity has time to do so. Radha had time to discover the personality of Krishna and vice versa. They couldn't forget each other. After a gap of many decades Radha saw Krishna at Kurukshetra. Radha told her friends—"There's no change in Krishna. He is the same boy." Here Radha didn't talk about personality. She was talking about the person Krishna.

Dhritrashatra was unable to see any person. He was a blind not only by his eyes but he had lost his sense of judgment. On the basis of his physical deformity he was denied the throne of his kingdom, despite being an elder brother. He had affection for his younger brother, Pandu. But he couldn't digest the reality that Pandu was becoming a king. When Pandu abdicated the throne on his own, Dhritrashtra didn't let any opportunity to go in vain. He tried his best to consolidate his position. He was over indulged in the business of denying Yudhishthira, the lawful successor to the throne, the kingship. For this he had a nexus with **D** company (Duryodhana and his associates). D company acted under the influence of inhibitions. Hence, Duryodhana didn't accepted Krishna's offer to give Pandavas even the fiefdom of five villages. He announced that he would not concede even a point of needle to the Pandavas. Hence, it became clear that the War became inevitable.

Krishna had no hesitations and inhibitions, so he came to Duryodhana and dealt with him in clear terms. He didn't take care of D company's pain and pleasure but he tried his best to avoid the war. Talking in clear term is possible only for them who've overcome their hesitations and inhibitions. Ydudhishthira accepted all the demands of D company. He was in a hesitation from his beginning. In the first year of their study, all Kaurvas and Pandvas princes tried to learn the all chapters assigned to them guru Dronacharya. All did accordingly. But Yudhishthira didn't learn more than one sentence. At the time of examination the guru asked Yudhishthira regarding the completion of the task assigned to them. He answered boldly that he had learnt only one sentence. His answer turned Guru Dronacharya furious. He started beating Yudhishthira but the disciple bore the onslaught. At last guru himself tired and stopped beating. He asked—"Why didn't you become angry?" Yudhishthira answered in a quiet composed tone—"Master, the first sentence of the assignment was—one should control his anger." "I concentrated on this sentence only. I tried to control my anger and I did so. You've beaten me bitterly but didn't loose my mental peace." Guru became proud of the performance of his disciple and embraced him.

He had controlled his temperament up to such an extent that he forgot to oppose injustices even. But Bhima wasn't convinced by his attitude. He opposed wherever he found injustice.

Kaurvas had inhibitions and Yudhishthira had hesitations. Under the impression of inhibitions or hesitations meeting of persons wasn't possible. Hence, the war was inevitable. Lord Krishna enjoyed his life thoroughly because he had no inhibitions and hesitations. To enjoy your life please overcome these two words. But overcoming these two words doesn't mean to be shameless and opposing our elders and respectable person. Today we're here because our parents gave birth to us, our teachers educated us and our family members love us. Hence, overcoming inhibitions and hesitations doesn't mean shameless boldness. It's to be integral and honest. To be dutiful and kind.

Krishna had no hesitations and inhibitions but he was possessed with all the humane qualities. Jingoist won't make any point anywhere. Overcoming inhibitions and hesitation is presenting "what is" as "what is." Krishna did so and we can also do so. Try once. For this one will have to overcome many other demerits and vested interests. It's difficult but not impossible. Many corporate gurus have made this possible in their life.

21. Be Innocent, Not Ignorant

तमुवाच हृषीकेशः प्रहसन्निव भारत।
सेनयोरूभयोर्मध्ये विषीदन्तमिदं वचः॥

- गीता

Tamuvach Hrishikeshah Prahasannamiva bharat Senayorubhayormadhye vishidantamidam Vachah

– *From* ***'Geeta'***

Meaning: *O Dhritarashtra, then Lord krishna said this to depressed Arjuna , with a smile amidst the Armies ready to fight.*

Innocence is divine but ignorance is a demerit. When I state this statement, I'm aware of an other statement by a renowned thinker. He said–"ignorance is bliss." I went into a deeper level of the statement by the thinker. I found that his intention was different. Actually he wanted to state that human beings are deeply engaged in facts and figures. Facts and figures robe away our humanity from us. They deviate us from the very pleasure of our life. Life becomes mechanical. We dwell on the very peripheries of the life. We remain away from the centre. Hence, he wanted to say that those who've no knowledge of facts and figures are ignorant. Such ignorance is bliss. I agree.

But knowledge is different thing. The thinker had limited the word ignorance as the opposite of information. But from information to wisdom there is processing.

Information ......after processing becomes knowledge. And knowledge ...after processing becomes wisdom. Information having future relevance is knowledge. And the knowledge that is eternal is wisdom. After attaining wisdom one becomes enlightened. To achieve enlightenment is blissful. Ignorance is opposed to enlightenment. Thus, ignorance is unwanted. Innocence is something beyond the duality of ignorance and enlightenment. An enlightened person can be innocent but an enlightened soul can't be ignorant. A man without enlightenment can be innocent too. But one should be wise and innocent simultaneously. It's very difficult. Knowledge brings a sense of vanity in an ordinary fellow. But a truly wise fellow sheds his pride and dwell in the paradise of innocence.

Lord Krishna was a treasure of knowledge and wisdom. But his innocence was infectious. The entire Braja region was under the sweet shadow of his innocence. Yashoda never believed that her son Krishna was naughty. She lived a life in the eternal love of Krishna and spent her entire life in his sweet memory. Krishna's innocence was her food for life.

This was the case of his foster mother, Yashoda. What about his actual parents? When he killed Kansa and came to meet his parents first time, they didn't believe that the same tender boy had killed a wicked demon king Kansa. They started weeping at their loss. They had repentance that they couldn't enjoy the childhood of their son. Krishna also became emotional. His parents forgot that the same boy was regarded as the lord almighty. This is called love. In such a love people forget status. Where there's status, there's decorum, there's respect, there's reverence. But love is above all such things.

Krishna forgot that Radha was a girl from a locality. And Radha forgot that Krishna was the supreme God, too. In love people become innocent. They lost their identity. Love is a process of killing 'I'. It shapes this 'I' to be more inclusive, broad and accepting. In love our acceptance grows. In love our receptivity grows. His male friends were even teasing him. They were aware of his almighty nature but they were innocent too. There was no curtain between the Lord and his friends. They were playing at the same level. Innocence provides us a level to enjoy the true person.

Lord Krishna advocated a synergy between wisdom and devotion in his Gita. Wisdom and devotion go together only when there's innocence. His close persons regarded him more than their life breaths. But no one feared them. Vasudeva Krishna was always an intimate friend to all his associates.

Ignorance pushes man on the level of animals. An ignorant person has no conscience. He doesn't feel the beauty of life. His enjoyment is the enjoyment of a fool. His sentiment is guided by a mean circle. Because an ignorant person dwells in his limited world. All the demons sent by Kansa to kill Krishna were ignorant people. They were following the dictate of their wicked master. They had learnt only the art of killing innocent people. Their world was limited. An ignorant person is guided by animal instinct. Their world is limited to mundane needs. They didn't care higher goals.

In many cases, we find blind followers are ignorant people. They're born to obey someone's whims and fancies. Duryodhana was an ignorant person. He followed the ambition of his blind father Dhritrashtra and dictate of his wicked maternal uncle Shakuni. People move on a suicidal path under the spate of such level of ignorance.

To achieve innocence in life demands a cool and balanced attitude towards life. Only a cool and balanced person can be innocent. Shishupal continued to insult Krishna in the court of Indraprastha but he didn't loose his temper. Once, Krishna's finger was cut by the sharp rage of his own favorite weapon, Sudarshana Chakra. No one had an idea to take any immediate action. Draupadi tore a piece from her precious sari and put a bandage with that portion of her cloth on the bleeding spot. Miraculous ! Bleeding stopped. Krishna was impressed by the innocence of Draupadi. She didn't care her cloth. She took care of her Krishna. Lord was so much impressed by her innocence that he couldn't ignore the call of Draupadi at the time of need. He helped her when Dushasana was pulling her sari to make her nude in the midst of the court. The sinful intention of the D company's (which included Duryodhana, Dhritrashtra and Dushasana) wasn't fulfilled. If this could happen, it was impossible for the Pandavas to survive. They might have committed suicide.

Yudhishthira's acceptance of D company's proposal to play gamble was neither his ignorance or his innocence. It was an act of continuing wrong practice in the name of obedience. He treated his brothers and wife as his personal property. It's an example of insanity. To be eldest doesn't allow any one to treat in this manner. Here is a line between innocence and intentional mistake.

22. Be Playful

जातस्य हि ध्रुवो मृत्युर्ध्रुवं जन्म मृतस्य च।
तस्मादपरिहार्येऽर्थे न त्वं शोचितुमर्हसि॥

– गीता

Jatasya hi dhruvo mriturdhruvam janma mritasya
Tasmadpariharyarthe na tvam shochitumargasi

– *From* **'Geeta'**

***Meaning**: Those who are born will die. After death , there will be birth again. Hence , you shouldn't be sorrowful in performing your unavoidable duties.*

Life is full of pain and pleasure. In modern times, people have a lot of problem to establish themselves. Even in the 21st century we see children dying due to hunger and epidemic. Where there's hunger, there're diseases, there's poverty......... sobbing mothers, children working in mines and factories and loosing the golden period of their childhood for trifles......is it possible to lead a playful life. This is the fact from have-nots life. What about haves? They're in a continuous struggle for building more and more for their future generations. They're on a hunt mission. Many people are struggling for their survival ......many persons are fighting for consolidating their empires for the future ...... a future that is unseen ....some are carrying their corporal existence in the present but dwell in their past. No one living in his present. In such a scenario, is it possible to be playful?

In life some problems are at physical level and others are at psychological problems. There're other problems too. They're neither physical nor emotional. They're imposed problems. Imposed by society, family and culture so on .... some problems are at attitudinal. They're self created. They may touch the periphery of psychological problems. Physical problems can be cured by the joint effort of society and individual. The world order are bound to change for betterment, when poverty and hunger related problems would be minimal. Physical deformity will be controlled up to maximum extent with the advancement of medical science and technological progress. Rest of the problems can be cured by one's own endeavor.

There're someone who float with the flow of current. There're people who turn the tide in their favour. Yet, there's another category. There're some persons who neither flow with the current nor turn the tide in their favour. They simply sit and meditate. They concentrate on "what is." Even some of them think of "What should be." Those who never deviates their eyes from "what is" remain playful. This doesn't mean that they're idlers, sitting on the fence and waiting for a windfall. But they've understood the fact that the life is precious. It's very difficult to get another chance. So pleasure lies in "what is," not in "what should be." An individual can put his effort to achieve "what should be." No doubt he should do so. But for doing so, one shouldn't miss the available time and space. One can see a labour family working in scorching sun heat and coming to their thatched roof house in the evening, sitting together some moments together and then cooking together, taking dinner what they've. They've no psychological problems. Next morning they come out from their tiny settlements in the search of a fresh work, listen music through his mobile chord. We find a rhythm in their life. They don't have any health related problem. They enjoy their work. They find some playful moments in their life. In our offices, we find certain persons enjoying their duty with a great enthusiasm. They've a passion for work. But at the same time they doing all their works with dedication. They discharge their all responsibilities with the same intensity. They never miss to fulfill their task with perfection.

This is possible only when an individual takes life as a whole and enjoy its each moment. Lord Krishna took all the assignments of his like with a great smile. He was an epitome of mirthful life. He faced problems from the moments of his birth and continued to face hurdles till the end but he was always happy. One could see a smile on his lips all the time. When he was merely a baby of six days, a dreadful demon lady came to kill her. Incidentally the demon was killed. When villages saw the demon lying dead on a pool of blood, the baby Krishna was playing on the chest of the monster. There was no harm to the baby. There was a charming smile on his lips. His parents ran to the boy but having seen him smiling they forgot their fear and became elated. **If you smile, you don't smile for yourself only; you smile for all the people you face and all the people who watch you. One smile can change the life of thousands.**

What to talk of six days old baby? When Krishna was born, his father Vasudeva took him to Braja. The river Yamuna flows between Mathura and Gokul. Vasudeva had to cross the river. He took baby Krishna in an open lid basket and started crossing the river. It was rainy season. Suddenly water level of Yamuna started rising. The boy took his feet out of the basket and touched the rising water level. With the touch of his feet water level started receding. Miraculous! A naughty Krishna!

Playing with his childhood friends he faced many problems. Sometimes demons attached him. Sometimes natural calamities happened. No doubt some moments of delicacy also appeared there. Radha and other girls were providing great emotional touch to fighting Krishna. Here Krishna could find love and affection. Everyone of Vrindavan was in selfless love with him. He saw many waxing and waning phases in his life but never saw the dark side. He spent every moment of his life in a playful manner. One should understand that this is the moment. I should be here in this moment. If there is chaos in life at this moment, the next moment will be better. This is possible when I'll be in a better mood now. If I'm in a better mood now, this moment will be a better moment. The next moment will best moment and I'll remain playful in my entire life. Those who want to bring a change in their life, should be playful. Lord Krishna led a playful life. Hence, he could bring many changes in human life. He was playful even at the time of war. On the basis of his playfulness he could deliver his Gita message in the battle field. This is unique in the history of mankind. The book like Gita could be delivered in the battle field. One can guess Krishna's playfulness.

During the war period, he performed the duty of chariot driver. He performed his duty with utmost dedication. He was respectable among the then kings and princes of Indian subcontinent but he took a job of very lower level during the war. From the bottom level he changed the course of history. One can bring change at the place where he works. To bring change one doesn't need to be at the helm of affair. Mahatma Gandhi started a movement on the basis of truth and non-violence in South Africa, at the time he wasn't a celebrity. In 1946 during communal riots, he used to pacify people through his unique method but in the night he had no problem in a sound sleep. This is a playful life. There's no contradiction between living a playful life while being a dutiful fellow. During Mahabharata war he used to serve his horses, clean their wounds, fulfill diplomatic assignments, chalk strategies and take time to play flute. He never forgot to play flute. It was the part of his life. This is a playful life. Work is important but hobby is also important. Duty is important but regular yoga is equally important. Office is important but family is more important. Work is more important but life is most important.

Krishna performed a lot of tasks in his life but he never forgot to fulfill his duty as a husband, as a son, as a father, as a member of the society and so on....... There must be a music in life, there must a rhythm in life. Situations come and go but the lost moments of life are never regained. There's no place for regret in life for those who're playful. Dedication is important, artificial seriousness is unwanted. Dedication in each moment. Smile in each moment and adopt playfulness in each moment.

If my surrounding isn't in my favour and I'm caught in a difficult situation for which I'm responsible or not, I won't let myself down. I'll change it with a smile, in a playful manner. That's all. I'll be playful for myself and for this world too. Lord Krishna was playful with his means. I'll be playful with my means. Take this mantra and enjoy your life. You'll feel a change at all levels in your life ......be it your body, family or office. We change, the world changes. Have a smile for Krishna's sake, for this author's sake and above all for yourself. Certainly your inner is waiting for you since your childhood. Allow some drops of honey fall on your inner......let is wet ...let it sing......let it dance ....let flowers bloom there ....let birds twitter there.......... Be playful!

Dha ...dhink ......dhin ...dha......Lord Krishna is playing flute ....you're playing it too.

23. Life Is Not a Bed of Roses

प्रसादे सर्वदु:खानां हानिरस्योपजायते।
प्रसन्नचेतसो ह्याशु बुद्धिः पर्यवतिष्ठते।।

– गीता

Prasade sarvaduhkhanam hanirsyopjayate
Prasannachetso hyashu budhih paryavatishthe

– *From* ***'Geeta'***

Meaning*: By the grace of Almighty a blessed person's all miseries get removed. In this stage of contentment , man gets a blissful equanimity.*

There's a legend of seven blind men. They were ordered to describe an elephant. To describe the elephant, they touched it one by one. One of the blind persons touched its trunk and said that elephant was like a serpent. Another from the lot touched it's feet and said that elephant was like a pillar. As per their experiences they described the shape of an elephant. But no one could describe the actual elephant. Hence, we look at the certain aspects of a thing and form our perception accordingly. We've a partial image of any thing. We look at a tree but while looking many ideas cross through our mind. They cast their shadow on our perception. We don't see a thing as it is.

We've already images in our mind created and imposed by the family, society, nation, religion, school, culture, linguistic groups, regional aspirations and so on.... The real man never gets a birth. Bodies come here and grows with other's perception. Bodies die with other's perception. Never enjoys "what is." Is this a life? Whether one looks at the negative aspect of life or at the positive aspect but that is not a life. It's away from reality. For someone life is a thorny path.

And there pangs, tears, sorrow, violence, misery, hunger and diseases in life. There's no mild breeze, there's no flower, no beauty in life for them. If flowers bloom, they bloom for others. If peacocks dance, they dance for others. If clouds shed raindrops, they do so for others. They don't find even a single dew drop falling on their barren land. This is a perception of a man who belongs to the lot similar to that of seven blind men.

There's a different lot. A person from this lot comes and says—"I've seen flowers blooming, peacock dancing, clouds raining, beautiful girls smiling, farmers cultivating, dew drops falling......I've enjoyed my life ...I'm enjoying it ......I'll enjoy it ......there'll be rainfall again ......there'll be dance of peacocks again ......flowers will bloom ...beauties will smile......there's no problem in my life ......Whatever seems a hurdle I solve it with my understanding. I solve my problems with my thinking. There are I and the thing but there's no problem. I've no partial vision, no particular attitude. I see the thing as it is. That's all. My life is a bed of roses."

Have you seen such a person in your life? If yes, then be inspired. If not, then, be yourself such a guy. In any case, it needs a transformation. Krishna delivered his Gita message for the transformation of Arjuna's life. After this sermon, the way life of Arjuna changed. No one else could perceive the change in that moment. He had same body and same situation. Before this sermon, he was in the midst of battle field. He was with Lord Krishna. He was in a dejected mood. After receiving the Gita message he was in the battle field. He was with Lord Krishna. But dejection was no where.

There was Arjuna, a changed Arjuna. Some hours of discourse changed his life thoroughly. He became a transformed Arjuna. There was no thorn on his path, despite being in the battle field. There were roses in his life. He killed many mighty warriors in the battle field. He survived the sorrowful moments after the death of his son Abhimanyu. The Gita is a message for transformation. The transformation happens only after understanding. Krishna makes you aware, makes you careful, makes you playful. He brings back an escapist Arjuna in the battle field. He delivers the message that life isn't an escape from reality but it's an enjoyment of reality. It's not meant weeping and crying. It's celebration. It's a meditation.

Be in a festive mood to celebrate it. His brother Balrama becomes serious, his wives become serious, Pandavas become serious but no one finds a serious Krishna. People find a loving Krishna, an affectionate Krishna, a warrior Krishna, a Krishna doing miraculous acts, doing divine acts, a Krishna smiling always. When at the end life, a hunter shot an arrow at his one foot, he didn't loose his calmness. There was peace in his heart. There was smile on his lips even in the moment of death.

Death is the culminating point of life. If you've led a transformed life, you'll enjoy the same status even in the moment of death. Death isn't a disintegrated episode of life. It's the last episode of life. Krishna led thinking and understanding life.

Hence, the life was a bed of roses for him. It's a bed of roses for a thinking man.If sorrow is to come, let it come. If pain is come, let it come. If you can change, change it. You can't change unforeseen moments. Let those moments come. Why to think for the negative moments?

Why to think death and destruction. Your positive tendencies may change tragedy into a mirthful event, a memorable moment, a soothing moment. Most of the people disturb their present in the name of past. Most of the people live under the shadow of fear.

Demons used to attack Krishna during playing and cattle grazing but he didn't leave playing and singing with friends.

He didn't leave dancing and playing with innocent girls of Braja. He had no hangs over of the past. He never led a life under the shadow of future. But he was careful. He was smart. He had understanding of his world. He had understanding of time and space.

An understanding guy excels in life. A smart guy succeeds. A careful guy faces calamities and danger with a smile. Thus life is a bed of roses for such a guy.

24. Moving on a Virgin Path

सदास्वरूपसम्प्राप्तः सर्वज्ञो नित्यनूतनः।
सच्चिदानन्दसान्द्रांगः सर्वसिद्धिनिज़ेवितः॥

– भक्तिरसामृतसिन्धु

Sadasvaroopsampraptah sarvajno nityanootanah
Sachchidanandsandrangah sarvasiddhihnishevitah

– *From **'Bhaktirasamritasindhu'***

***Meaning**: Lord krishna is beyond the grasp of illusion. He is omniscient. He is ever new. He is the eternal bliss and lord of all divine powers.*

Krishna was born in a prison in Mathura. He killed a lady demon on the sixth day of his birth. He killed hundreds of demons before achieving the age of twelve. He killed demon king Kansa at the same age. He went to sage Sandipani's traditional school and learnt all arts in sixty four days only. He fought many wars with Jarasandha. He kept Govardhan mountain on his little finger for seven days. He was a great thinker, great warrior, musician, singer, dancer and above all master of sixty four arts. He delivered the Gita in the battle field of Mahabharata. After acquiring international fame in his life time, he accepted the task of chariot driver of Arjuna. He gave patronage to sixteen thousand girls captured by a wicked king. He freed them and gave them shelter in his kingdom. He left the kingdom of Mathura for the peace of the region and founded a new kingdom Dwarka on the bank of Arabian sea.

Lord Krishna fought with a highly poisonous snake named Kalia in his childhood and put his effort to make Yamuna clean. So many extraordinary task performed by a single person! Wonderful! People wonder and say—is it possible to fulfill so many tasks by a single individual? No doubt Krishna led an extraordinary life and he performed many extraordinary tasks.

Besides Krishna, there have been many persons in the history of mankind who performed extra ordinary tasks. Some one says—"Krishna has done it, I'll do it. Buddha has done it, I'll do it. Chanakya has done it, I'll do it. Henry Ford has done it, I'll do it. Newton has done it, I'll do it. Gandhi has done it, I'll do it. Bill Gates has done it, I'll do it." Certainly he can do it. But he can't repeat the same thing. If you're going to repeat it, you won't be successful. Nothing is repeated. You can get inspiration from them and chalk your own strategy. One can move on a well trodden path, one can get benefit on it and loss on it but one can't create a phenomenon by moving on it. Those who created a new thing by moving on a virgin path. They made a path for himself. All the above mentioned names are phenomena. They aren't individuals now. Their life and deeds have become possession of public domain. They're the ever burning lights to show a way to mankind. They're inspiration for the mankind. They're relevant for all time.

Bill gates was a school drop out. But he created a world renowned organisation, Microsoft. After making it a mega company and spreading its product and activity world wide, he relinquished the post of chairman. Now he and his wife Melinda are actively engaged in philanthropic activities. Do all school drop outs perform such a task? Gandhi followed the path of truth and non-violence. It was a great experiment in the field of politics. Gandhi thought and dared to do so.

Krishna delivered his Gita lecture in the battlefield. This was first experiment in the history of mankind. This gave that war a higher significance. In the Gita we find some elements of Upanishad. This idea was prevalent before Krishna but Krishna added something new to it. He presented it in a new style. Here tradition met with individual talent. One can perform similar action but one can't deliver anything like the Gita in the battlefield. From where any one can arrange the Mahabharata war? From where any can bring the Kauravas and Panadavas? Hence, the situation is different. Characters are different.

We're living in a different world. Here we're facing different types of demand. Our life situation is different. Mode of production has been changed. Hence, those who're willing do something new, they must choose a virgin path created by themselves. Self created path can lead them to their destination. No doubt, there will be Krishna's inspiration and blessings of many more. Source of inspiration may be many but the creator will be one, the man who strives to achieve a new height.

Krishna utilised traditional weapons in the war but he inspired Arjuna to acquire something new by pleasing different gods. What is already known is with many persons. They're in the help of many. No doubt, they'll be helpful. But those who want to excel will have to find something new for himself. There will be Krishna again. There will be no another Gita again.

Every particle has an independent identity in this universe. Nothing is the photocopy of the other. A photocopy is a photocopy. It has lost the glaze of original. You're a separate individual. You can move on others path. You'll be a follower. Following a good idea or a good thing is always beneficial. One should support whatever good and beautiful in this world. But creation is unique thing. Many persons has written books on "Management Guru" on great personalities but repeating the same thing won't make a book. If you don't find any new interpretation in this book, it won't be a book ......It will be a tautology. Here words are moving because the author feels that something new is going on.

One can't survive without assimilating the important aspects our tradition but to create a new thing one will have to chisel something new. One needs a new design to create a virgin path. To sale a new product, you need new stuff and new packaging. With new packaging, you need a new slogan, a new bottom line to sale the item. After launch and finding a new foot hold in the market, the survival of the product depends on its quality and stuff. People get satisfied by the quality, durability and service provided by the company. Then the particular make gets recognition.

Krishna is different from all the incarnations born before him. In the same way Buddha is different, Gandhi is different .... Difference makes one different. But only to move on a virgin path you can't move. Everybody can't be an innovator. Innovation should be in your blood. If you've an inborn instinct of an innovator, you must move on a virgin path. But if you don't have such an inborn instinct, you should follow the way designed by others. Krishna devised strategy and many followed on that path.

Krishna jumped into the river Yamuna to fight with Kalia. But no other boys of Braja jumped into the river because all had the estimate of their respective capacity. Krishna raised Govardhana hill on his little finger and saved his people from the onslaught of heavy rain. People watched and praised him but no one followed his way. They were wise people. Nothing is impossible but one must have strength to do the impossible. One's capacity is increased, strength is enhanced but one should estimate before the action.

If an individual isn't an astronaut, how can he go for a space odyssey? If an individual isn't an army personal, how can he go to fight on the frontier? No doubt, everyone's duty is to protect his frontier but it is in emergency situation. This can't be a rule. First understand yourself, your capacity, your aspiration, your driving force, your skill and the understand the prevalent go of the industry.

After doing your home work thoroughly you can concentrate on your individual demand and the aspiration of the society. If you've gone into such a deeper level, you will discover the pearl from the sea bed. Rest is yours. Krishna had all things and he catered the need of the society. Thus, he moved on a virgin path. Rest of the society followed him and sang his song. People are singing nowadays.....they are chanting......Krishna, Govinda, Gopala, Muralidhara,

Madhava ....We listen to songs and mantras to please him. Hope to listen in future also. His Gita is relevant even today and it'll continue to do so. Though its interpretation will change from time to time. Time will change and singers will change but the Gita will be same and Krishna will remain the same.

25. Apathy, Sympathy and Empathy

यं हि न व्यथयन्त्येते पुरुषं पुरुषर्भः।
समदुःखसुखं धीरं सोऽमृतत्वाय कल्पते॥

– गीता

Yam hi na vyathayantyete purusham purusharabha
Samdukhasukham dheeram so amritatvaya kalpate

– *From* ***'Geeta'***

Meaning: *O Arjuna, those who are not get disturbed by the duality of pain and pleasure , are sure to achive a blissful stage in life.*

There're accidents in our daily life. There's a chaos in the system. Someone dies on a roadside but no one cares to save him. Corrupt politicians run a country but people vote for him again and again. It doesn't mean that all the people in the country have become corrupt. They've apathy.

Someone comes to save people and help them. Some people do philanthropic activities. There're many persons who come forward to help needy fellows. They've sympathy for others. There's apathy in this world. There's sympathy in this world. At the same time there is empathy in this world too. A devotee named Kashim donated a horse to Shirdi Saibaba. One day an attendant started beating the horse. After some moments, Saibaba told a person to save the horse. Normally one can think that this was a case of sympathy but it was more than that. When the person returned to Saibaba, he saw his back was bleeding profusely. This was a case of empathy. Baba took on himself the misery faced by the horse. We find similar incident in the life of Lord Ramakrishna Paramhansa. A landlord was supposed to come to see Lord Paramhansa. For this he had to cross the Ganges. It was feared that a storm could occur at any moment. He ordered a boat man to sail across the river. The boatman refused to do so. Having done so, he was beaten bitterly by the landlord. After this the land lord managed another boat man. Anyhow, he came to meet Paramhansa. But Ramakrishna refused to see him. When he enquired of the reason, the god man showed him his back. It was bleeding profusely. Ramakrishna took a wound of all his hunters on his back and saved the boatman. This was a case of empathy.

When you've no feeling for anyone, it's apathy. It's indifference. When you've a kind feeling for someone, it's sympathy. If you've the same feeling of a sufferer, it's empathy.

Lord Krishna's entire life was an example of empathy. In this regard, there're many interesting tales. One day, after a separation of many years, Radha met Krishna. When all went to take rest in their camps in the night, Lord said his beloved wife Rukmini to send a glass of mild hot milk for Radha because Radha had a habit of taking a glass of milk before sleep. How caring was Lord Krishna? He couldn't forget the habits of his childhood friend, Radha. So intense love! So intimacy! Rukmini followed the order and came back soon because she had to take care of the Lord also. In the morning she woke up and saw the feet of Krishna. There was swelling in his feet. She summoned the royal physician to cure the swelling but Krishna refused to take medicine. He said—"Radha meditate my feet in his heart. In the last night you sent a glass of burning hot milk to Radha in haste and said that it was sent by Krishna. She too took the glass in haste, believing it an offering from me. She felt heart burn. In this way, I also felt the burnt in my feet and also the swelling." Rukimini felt very sorry but she wanted the swelling to be cured. She asked Krishna to suggest a remedy.

Krishna told her—"If any woman, who loves me, touches her feet on my chest, I'll be cured." No wife was ready to do so, including Rukmini. Touching Lord by feet would be a sinful act. When Radha got the news, she became ready to touch his chest by her feet. She told—"I'm ready to accept sin on my head but my prime concern is Krishna's well being." She came and touched Krishna. His swelling disappeared. This is love. This is empathy, love from both sides. This is empathy from both sides.

In the tense moments of the Mahabharata war, Bhishma shot many arrows towards Arjuna. He had to resist Bhishma. Lord Krishna took a wheel in his hands and rushed towards Bhishma. The great warrior Bhishma honoured him and saluted him. Then, he returned to his chariot. Krishna had taken a vow that he wouldn't take any weapon in his hands during the War but for protecting his horses and friend (Arjuna), he had to take a wheel in his hand. This is empathy.

Krishna liberated his parents from the prison of Kansa and for this, he could have given Kansa free life. But it would have been a personal deal. He had empathy for the entire society. He wanted to liberate the entire community from the tyrannical rule of Kansa. Such a person doesn't live life for personal gain. Such a person lives a life for the mankind. Jesus didn't accept his death for his personal gain. He lived for his disciples and died for them. Buddha met his demise for the pleasure of his devotee, Chanda. He offered the Lord a dish made from pork. After eating the unhygienic meat dish, the Buddha had loose motions and later, he met his end. But he had empathy for his devotee.

Sympathy may change with the change of time and situation but empathy is a divine thing. Growth of an individual in necessary but an individual grows with the growth of society. The employee, who has empathy for his organisation, lives for it, thinks for it and works for it, is a vital part of his organisation. Such dedicated staff is an asset for organisations. A good boss should take care of such staff and do something needful for the growth of such staff. Arjuna thought about Krishna and loved him. So, Krishna took care of all his well being. A disciple takes care of his guru and serves him with utmost dedication. For this the guru takes care of material as well as spiritual advancement of the disciple. A guru has empathy for his disciple. Management Guru Lord Krishna had empathy for his world. To make his world clean and righteous, he took a weapon in his hands. To make it lovely, he loved everyone. He tried to beautify it and adore it.

When his friend Sudama came to seek help, he could not speak even a single word due to his hesitation. But Krishna had empathy for his friend. He honoured the feeling of his friend. He didn't say a single word that could signify his cry for help. After some days of royal hospitality, Sudama returned from Dwarka; he was empty handed. When he reached his native place, he saw a palace on the very spot of his house. When he enquired about the whereabouts of his hut, he was told that Lord Krishna had got a palace built on that very spot for his friend, Sudama. This is empathy. Empathy widens our horizon. It makes our personality acceptable to the most.

Lord Krishna is called the god of love. He loved all the creatures. He wanted to help all those who remembered him. His help was beyond the level of sympathy. It was on the level of empathy. For empathy an incarnation announces – "I'm with all. I'm in all." Lord Krishna also declared in his Gita – "Nothing is beyond me. This world is in me. And I'm in this world." Empathy makes one integral. On such a stage of unity we say a person synonymous to an organisation/nation/society. Narayana Murthy has become synonymous with Infosys. Bill Gates has become synonymous to Microsoft. Krishna dwells in the heart of his devotees. His devotees dwell in him. Thus, empathy is humane and beyond. It's divine. It turns mundane into divine.

26. If Wishes Were Horses...

यस्त्विन्द्रियाणि मनसा नियम्यारभतेऽर्जुन।
कर्मेन्द्रियैः कर्मयोगमसक्तः स विशिष्यते॥

– गीता

Yastvaindriyani mansa niymyarbhate Arjuna
Karmendriyaih karmayoga saktah sa vishishyate

– From ***'Geeta'***

Meaning*: Those faithful persons who put their endeavor to command over all their senses and mind and perform the yoga of action without any lust , are great persons.*

If wishes were horses every one ride on them. Man thinks to touch stars. There's no crime in being unable to touch stars but having no dream to touch stars isn't a welcome act. This isn't a statement to make human beings unnecessarily ambitious but it's a statement to inspire people to harness their potential to a maximum extent. But every one can't ride of the horses of wishes. For this one needs to be capable.

One point is common in all successful personalities. This is their practical approach. They think on an upper level but works on the ground level. To work in the field one needs pragmatic approach. He needs to understand people's need and sentiment. First of all, we need to understand ourselves. Understanding oneself, is the understanding of the world. Krishna understood his world. He understood his time. He understood the world order prevalent in his time. He was well aware of the purpose of his incarnation and worked accordingly.

After the death of Kansa, his father-in-law, Jarasandha, attacked Mathura. Krishna faced the challenge and compelled Jarasandha to return. But Jarasandha was unwilling to submit. He continued to harass the innocent subjects of Mathura. People had already suffered a lot during the tyrannical regime of Kansa. Krishna wasn't in the mood to bear any further injury inflicted upon the innocent people. Hence, he considered a different option. He convinced elders of Mathura to shift their kingdom to Dwarka. They voted in Krishna's favour. He could kill Jarasandha easily but he adopted a pragmatic approach. It was a difficult decision. Mass migration was to take place. People had to leave their native place. They had to leave their land and immovable properties. It was a loss to economy besides emotional loss. But all decided in favour of Krishna because they thought that Krishna wouldn't take any imaginary decision. He wouldn't allow his wishes to fly in an uncontrolled manner. He was omniscient.

He founded his kingdom (Dwarka) at a strategic location. Dwarka was on the sea shore of India. It was founded on the western sea coast, Arabian sea coast. It was meeting point between the south and the north. It was on an important trade route. From the very beginning of its foundation Dwarka flourished as a rich state. It's trade and commerce flourished with a geometrical progression. Neighbouring states become envious to its prosperity. But Krishna didn't waste his time to indulge into the luxury of his kingdom. He had fulfill the very purpose of his incarnation.

Rukmini wanted to marry him but her brother had a different plan. She sent a letter to Lord Krishna and expressed her desire to marry him. She sought Krishna's help. A woman willing to get a husband of her choice, unwilling to marry a wicked person imposed by her family members. It was the question of woman's right. It was a revolutionary step in the time. When in the 21st century lovers are murdered and face social stigma, it was a difficult choice. But Krishna was a revolutionary. He supported anything that was true and relevant to human rights. By the effort of such great souls India touched its golden height. Its glory inspires people even today. Krishna thought that he wouldn't abduct the lady but he would respect her desire and fulfill her wish. For this he waited Rukmini outside a temple. She came there with her friends. In the presence of Rukmini's, Krishna accepted her hands in marriage. When her brother chased them, he fought her beloved brother. Krishna defeated her brother but didn't take his life. He respected the sanctity of blood relation. Here he adopted a pragmatic approach. But he didn't fulfill the desire of every one to be his spouse. There were thousands of girls in his time who were willing to marry him. But he didn't fulfill the desire of all. Draupadi was also in love with him much before her marriage. But Krishna made it very clear that she would be good friend of him. She would be his life long friend but not wife. Draupadi had no demerit. She was beautiful, smart, meritorious, learned and so on. But Krishna thought that Draupadi would be a good wife to Pandavas. Only she could keep Pandavas united. The survival of Pandavas was essential for making a righteous society. It was essential for the future of India. Hence, he convinced Draupadi and remain her life long friend. His wishes weren't horses.

A manager takes a pragmatic decision. He isn't swayed by his whims and fancy. He doesn't allow his personal attitude prevail over his judicious faculty. He keeps his conscience clear. Lord Krishna had penetrating eyes. He did what he believed. He was very objective in his approach. Draupadi and Bhima weren't in a mood to have any communication with the Kauravas just before the Mahabharata war. They had a clear idea that the messenger would be insulted and it would be taken as the weakness of Pandavas. They were right on their own right. But Krishna had to seek another option to avoid the war. A responsible person should avoid war at any cost. Krishna didn't miss this opportunity despite knowing the outcome. He was well aware of the nature of Kauravas but life and property of millions of people were more important that fulfilling the vow of certain people, fulfilling the desire of some people and giving a position to whims and fancy of some people. He went their and returned without any result. He didn't prevail his desire over the cause of welfare of masses.

A good manager thinks about the welfare of his organisation first. He doesn't allow his subjectivity prevail over general welfare. Every person has certain likes and dislikes. But one should control his pluses and minuses to achieve a success. Success demands sacrifice. Lord Krishna sacrifice his childhood love. He had to bear the separation of Radha because he had to do many things for the world. He had an intense love with Radha. Such a love demands all the time. A lover's entire existence is submerged in such a love. Krishna was a multi dimensional incarnation. He was the master of all arts. He didn't allow his love to die. He had the same feeling for his Radha till the end. But he didn't allow his love to prevail over his other activities.

A smart manager has a balance life. He doesn't allow his family life to influence his office activities. For this one needs harmony in his home and good relation in his society.

Part IV

Management Guru Lord Krishna and Solution for International Conflict

27. War and Peace

क्लैब्यं मा स्म गमः पार्थः नैत्तत्त्वय्युपपद्यते।
क्षुद्रं हृदयदौर्बल्यं त्यक्त्वोत्तिष्ठ परन्तप॥

– गीता

Kavalyam ma sma gamah parthah naittattvayyupapdyate Kshudram hridyadaurbalyam tyakttvottishtha parantap

– *From* ***'Geeta'***

***Meaning**: O Arjuna don't be effeminate. This doesn't suit you. O destroyer of foes relinquish your weakness and stand up to fight a war for the victory of truth.*

During the last three millennium human beings have fought more than six thousand wars. On the basis of such a barbarism, are we qualified to be called human beings? But war is in the blood of human beings. It seems that human beings have been sent here for the purpose of fighting. Life has no goals. Perhaps it's encoded in our DNA to seek an opportunity of war. Where's tolerance? Where's non-violence? Where's peace? Of course, we talk of them a lot. But should we ask this question to ourselves? Whether we are civilised or barbarous? No doubt, we don't kill other human beings for their flesh, barring the example of Idi Amin, the former dictator of Uganda. He ate flesh of some of his beloved and colleagues.

Whether we're civilised by killing people in the name of

religion? We find bigotry and fundamentalism increasing day by day even in the 21st century. People spread terrorism in the name of religion. Actually, a true religion has nothing to do with fundamentalism. It has no business with terror. A true religion inspires a person to move on the path of spiritualism and to make this a beautiful place. It inspires mankind to have trust in the entire existence.

Anything that debases the dignity of any human being can't be called religion. A religion gives our heart a new height. It can't advocate terrorism. This world is full of diversity. The survival of human civilisation depends on recognition of others' cultures, values and faith. No one can move this world in a particular direction.

Psychology of war is more complex. It's not based on a single idea. Sometimes people fight because they're afraid of others. Sometimes, they fight to enjoy their privileges. Sometimes, they fight to eliminate people belonging to a different belief. Sometimes, they grab the property and women of others. Sometimes, they fight to destroy a civilisation. Sometimes, they fight for the annihilation of a culture. Christians are afraid of Muslims. Hindus are afraid of Christians and Muslims. Muslims are afraid of other religious communities. The Hindu faith was prevalent in Afghanistan two thousand years ago.

Then Buddhism an offshoot from Hinduism took its root in Afghanistan. Later followers of Islam controlled this land. In the end of twentieth century Taliban had command over Afghanistan. They demolished the famous Bamiyan Buddhist site. It was an important trade point in Ancient India. Many famous travellers visited India through this route.

Osama bin Laden motivated his men to attack the World Trade Centre in the U.S.A. Thousands of innocent people died in that attack. After a decade of this accident, under the leadership of its President (Barrack Obama), the U.S.A. captured Osama bin Laden, who was hiding in Pakistan. Terrorism is an international problem. India has been victim of terrorism.

In Sri Lanka, we've witnessed a bloody racial war that took the life of millions. India is a multi-racial, multi-lingual country full of geographical and cultural diversity. Its diversity lies in its assets.

The world has fought two world wars in which millions of soldiers and civilians were killed. Sometimes, people fight in the name of religion. Sometimes, they fight in the name of nationality. Sometimes, they clash in the name of culture. Sometimes, they fight due to fear. But territory and religion have been a great cause of war.

In the pastoral community in the prehistoric time, there was no war in the name of religion and territory. But when human beings started agriculture, fight for territory began. States came into existence. War of capturing other's territory began. During Krishna's time, D company wasn't ready to give even an inch of territory without fighting a war, although Pandavas were the lawful successors of the throne.

Righteous people should be tolerant but sometimes, criminals take good persons' tolerance otherwise. Hence, to maintain social order, even the good has to take weapons.

Kansa had a fear for his life. He believed in a forecast that the eight son of Devaki would kill him. On the basis of this forecast he started committing crimes against the people of Braja where Krishna was believed to be. Kansa was a wicked king and he had given patronage to all anti social elements of his time. There was a continuous fight among different states. There were external threats too. Kalayavan was from a country situated to the west of Indian sub continent. He was a continuous threat to the sovereignty of India. Krishna killed him very tactfully. He showed the way that sometimes we should seek solution without arms. When Kansa invited him to Mathura, the very purpose of Kansa was to kill him. He went there without any arm. He behaved friendly with the people of Mathura.

He loved Kubja, an innocent lady having hunched back. But when he reached the ground where a festival was to be held, Kansa's men started attacking him. He had to protect himself. In this process, he had killed Kansa's men. In the end Kansa was also killed. Krishna tried his best to convince the Kauravas to live peacefully with Pandavas. But Kaurvas weren't ready for any agreement. Ultimately, the War of Mahabharata was fought. But we've seen the war isn't a solution. For solution one has to initiate dialogue. But human beings haven't learnt the art of not accepting the things that don't belong to them. Only contentment is the solution to war. Contentment must be in the blood of human beings. But violence is in the blood of human beings.

Our aggression has annihilated many creatures from the earth. Many other creatures are on the verge of extinction. In the coming time, it's feared that many more will disappear from this world. Many species of plants are to disappear.

During the time of Babar, there were 1500 hundred variety of paddy were found in India. Now it's not more than one hundred. Man has destroyed bio-diversity. Even modern pattern of development and management education push man to be more aggressive, more violent and ever greedier. Competitiveness makes us more aggressive. There's no true co-operation. What should an individual do in such a circumstance?

Krishna's Gita message is the answer. In the Gita, Lord said—"You can't escape from fight. But fight for a good cause. Fight for justice. You must struggle to make yourself a spiritual person. Fight for the liberation of mankind." Nelson Mandela fought for the liberation of the black in South Africa. Gandhi fought for the millions in India. Buddha fought for the down trodden. One shouldn't fight for spreading terrorism and racial feeling.

There is no end of war till we don't respect other's faith, other's religion, other's territory and other's property. In a company stooges try to push out a genuine person. But if the boss is like Dhritrashtra, he pays heed to stooge like Shakuni. But the boss is like Krishna, he makes a team of efficient personnel. And he wins a war.

If you support a corrupt person or a corrupt organisation, whatever is your problem, you'll have to meet your end like Bhishma and Dronacharya. If you've faith in yourself, your god, your boss and your company, no one will stop you from success. Krishna formed a team. They fought together and won together. Unite for a good cause, be it war or peace. War and peace are the parts of our life. We are compelled to fight a war. War isn't our choice. Peace is our choice.

Try to embrace the latter, at personal, social, organisational or national level.

28. Freedom and Taboos

सर्वधर्मानपरित्यज्य मामेकं शरणं व्रज।
अहं त्वां सर्वपापेभ्यो मोक्षयिष्यामि मा शुचः॥

– गीता

Sarva dharmanparityajya mamekam sharanam vraj
Aham tvam sarvaiapapebhyo mokshayishyami ma shuchah

– *From* ***'Geeta'***

Meaning: *After relinquishing all your waverings come to my shelter, I'll rlieve you from all your sins.*

Society should respect the feeling of an individual. And an individual should respect the norms of society. But this doesn't happen. Society makes norms but doesn't change them with the change of time. Nowadays, traditional society is on the verge of extinction all over the world. People try to conserve ancient values. But they're in a minority. Pace of development has become very fast. Traditional societies find it difficult to adjust with the pace of development.

Sometimes, we hear a fight in the name of marriage within the clan. Sometimes, we come across the news of honour killing because the girl and the boy belonged to two different communities. Sometimes, the son revolts against the father. Sometimes, we hear the news that a lady was paraded in the street without any clothes on her body. Such events are not new happenings. We find the description of such events in all points of history. Society and the state try regulate but individuals violate. But man needs a society and there's no concept of society without men.

Rules and norms are made for the benefit of society. But with the change of time certain norms become obsolete. But who will change these obsolete norms? The answer is—no one, except daring persons. Norms are violated often due to greed but occasionally in the name of need. People from certain areas formulated a norm that members within the same *gotra* won't marry. But now boys and girls from the same *gotra* marry. That's why we witness the cases of honour killing. I don't want to go into the merit or demerit of such incidents. But life is complex. There's no simple solution to all problems, we face or see. There're geographical and cultural variations.

In north India, marriage of a girl with her maternal uncle will be considered a crime but in south India such a marriage has high regard. In north India a lady keeps her vein on her head. It's a symbol of her enjoying a marital life. But in south India, this practice is supposed that her husband is dead. After the death of husband, the veil is put on the head of the widow. India Buddhists don't eat meat but outside India Buddhists eat meat. In Tibet lamas take meat because their geographical conditions have forced them to continue the practice of eating meat. In the plains of northern India, a woman marries only one husband. Here, polyandry is regarded as a crime but in the certain tribal communities of the north-east India polyandry is prevalent. In India, Hindus can't practice bigamy but in Islam a male can keep four wives. We can't say what is social or what is anti- social. We find members of dozens of communities living together is a single street in India. They interact with one another. Elders have no time to make their children aware of their respective distinct social norms and values. Perhaps most of them don't find any interest in such things. Students from different social groups go to a school. Usually, they don't talk their castes in their class rooms. They've more things to do—higher or mundane. They want to make their life playful. Members of opposite sexes come together, work together, dine together, dance together and sing together. Then where will be taboo.

This is present scenario. What about Krishna's time? Yes, certain things were prevalent in his time also. One day, the girls of Vrindavan were taking bath in the river Yamuna. Krishna robed their dresses kept on the bank. But this wasn't a mischief. He had to warn anti-social practices. Those girls were swimming in the river in a nude position. Being nude on a public place is a wrong thing. No one should promote such a thing. Nudity isn't accepted in a civilised society. Lord Krishna returned their clothes only after taking words from them for not committing such a thing again. In ancient India, such types of bathing practices were common. Krishna forced them to stop such a practice. Something unhealthy is also found in tradition.

Recently France passed a law where no woman is allowed to wear burqa. But members from Islam oppose it. They may have certain logic. They may cite some rules and examples from their religious books. No doubt, they've right to do. But it's regarded as an offence against the dignity of women in France. They've different social values. Like India, they're not ready to allow continuing all the practice in the name of religion. India is a soft State; here, everything is acceptable. Here, one can do whatever one likes. But during Krishna's time women had freedom to much extent. The *purdah* (veil on face) system wasn't prevalent in ancient India. It took place after the arrival of Islam. Today we object a lady wearing fewer clothes. But in Ancient India, normally a lady used to put fewer clothes, but it wasn't a vulgarity. Woman had freedom to love and marry a husband of her choice. Perhaps, it was more so in a royal community. We don't have data regarding a member of ordinary class.

There were negative taboos too. Except the Brahmins and Kshatriyas, people couldn't receive education. In the later phase, this facility was granted to members of Vaishya community because they were businessmen and indulged mostly in trading activities. They acquired huge wealth. Their wealth pushed them upward on the social ladder. A great warrior, whose name was Eklavya, was denied education (in the field of archery) because he was from a low-caste community. He showed his respect to Dronacharya. Guru Dronacharya took his thumb for his reverence and denied him off his skill of archery. But Ekalavya didn't succumb to such a trick. During the Mahabharata war, he came to fight with Arjuna, a favourite disciple of Dronacharya. Though he came from wrong side, Krishna praised him. Lord Krishna had a great respect for merit. He broke all the circles that continued to chain human beings. He enjoyed the company of ordinary village folk.

When Braja ladies came to dance with Krishna in a cool full-moon night on the bank of Yamuna, he forbade them to do so because he had a great respect for social values. He tried his best to convince them that a lady shouldn't stay with another man in a lonely place, that too in the night. But the ladies had clear conscience. They told him that they didn't regard him as a male but they regarded him as God. With such a high spiritual feeling they danced with Krishna but he never crossed the limit.

He married Rukmini only when she requested him and sought his help to rescue her from compelling to marry a criminal minded person. Here, the choice of elders was against the rights and emotions of an innocent beautiful lady. Krishna came forward and married her. In the case of Draupadi, he had to support polyandry. Draupadi, the daughter of Punjab, was a beautiful lady. She had a great respect for Lord Krishna. It was necessary to keep all the five Pandavas united. Hence, he supported Polyandry with the consent of Draupadi.

His own sister (Subhadra) was in love with Arjuna but his elder brother (Balrama) wanted her to marry Duryodhana. Duryodhana was a renowned wicked. Hence, Krishna motivated Arjuna and Subhadra to get engaged through love marriage to counter the strategy of Balrama. At last the elder brother had to give his consent. Arjuna was Subhadra's cousin brother. Kunti was Subhadra's father's sister. Arjuna was the son of Kunti. Lord Krishna promoted such a marriage.

When Kaurvas were trying to make Draupadi nude in the court of Dhritrashtra, Krishna protected her dignity. Sixteen thousand girls were imprisoned by the then king of Kamrupa. Krishna freed them and gave them his protection. No one could marry such girls because they were supposed to spend their time in prison. They weren't criminal girls. They were the daughters of kings and noble persons who were killed in war. The king of Kamrupa captured all orphan girls. Krishna gave them a great support. In this way he saved India from a great social unrest. He defeated the king and freed them. That was the peak of generosity. He did what he believed. His heart was always on the right place. Sometimes granting too much freedom to an individual may pose problems for the society. In some societies freedom is so uncontrolled that there's no society there. But in some societies, taboos are so strong that individual has to face a lot of problem, particularly women have no right there. Krishna was neither in favour granting anti-social freedom nor in support of taboos that violate human rights. The lack of such a balance results in many unnecessary problems at micro and macro levels.

29. Governance without Corruption

सत्त्वात्संजायते ज्ञानं रजसो लोभ एव च।
प्रमादमोहौ तमसो भवतोऽज्ञानमेव च॥

– गीता

Sattvatsanjayate jnanam rajso lobh eva cha
Pramadamohau tamso bhakto ajnan meva cha

– *From* ***'Geeta'***

Meaning: *Sattava gunas give true knowledge. Rajas breeds greed. And tamas gives ignorance, lethargy and illusion.*

Note : There are three qualities in this universe - sattava (righteous and spiritual) , rajas (mundane) and tamas(darkness and passivity).

Financial corruption spoils the entire system of governance. News of a corrupt person is flashed. It becomes sensation in media for some days. Like the change in seasons, people's mood gets changed. The corrupt is spared. At least, this phenomenon is repeated most of the time. Hence, members of any government and those of public have acquired immunity to such news.

Today, most of the countries of the world, suffer from such scandals. In India ministers in many governments committed crimes relate do to financial corruption. Not only many ministers have tainted past but bureaucrats and general public are also in the fray to amass wealth that belongs to others. Even corporate sector and private companies indulge in such crimes. Examples and data in this context go longer. Hence, citing names won't serve any purpose here. Other countries also face this problem.

What's the root of this global problem? This isn't a new device. In all historical point of time, we find examples of corrupt people. During the time of Krishna this problem was of subtle nature. Krishna handled this task with a professional manner.

Corruption means amassing the resources, by hooks and crooks, which belong to others. Earning through lawful means and paying taxes properly and discharging one's duty adequately is always welcome. Tendency to get other's belonging through improper means is an age long practice.

First of all, I would like to cite a beautiful example from Lord Krishna's time. He had many friends. Most of them became prosperous in due course of time. But the fortune of Sudama remained in doldrums; he was Krishna's most favourite friend. He had to undergo through severe problems. He had to sleep hungry many nights. What to talk of his meals, his wife and children had to spend days and nights without taking meals. He was a talented and righteous person. When one is possessed with these two qualities, one has to suffer a lot. In most of the cases people don't translate their righteousness into action. Their righteousness remains confined to their words only. But our Sudama Ji was made up of a different stuff.

Lord Krishna befriended him during his stay at Guru Sandipani's gurukula. In ancient times, schools used to be run by learned persons and they were known as Gurukulas. These schools weren't run by anyone for making profit. In such systems, all kinds of work used to be performed by students and the family of their guru. Students had to bring woods from nearby forest for cooking food besides doing other works. It was a self-help system.

One day the wife of guru Sandipani sent Krishna and Sudama to the forest for collecting wood logs. She gave Sudama a small packet of roasted grams. The quantity wasn't enough for two boys. During the course of completing the assignment, Sudama felt hunger. He was on the tree. Krishna was waiting him under the tree. Sudama was from a poor family. He had already suffered from hunger. Even on the tree, the packet of roasted grams was with him. As soon as felt hunger, he started eating the stuff. It might be possible, that the quantity wasn't enough to satisfy the both. But Sudama should have offered at least a portion from what he had to Krishna. When Krishna asked him—"What're you eating my friend?" He replied—"Nothing. I'm feeling severe cold. Hence, a hiss sound is emitting from my mouth." In fact, it was the sound of mastication of grams. In his childish mood, Sudama committed two mistakes. He ate other's share. And the second was—telling lie before his dearest friend. It was an unethical act. It affected the integrity of Sudama. Lord Krishna said nothing but smiled at the childish behavior of his friend.

In due course of time, this event had a great impact on Sudama. He went through a phase of repentance and emerged as an emblem of moral values after passing out of Sandipani's gurukula. He didn't move even a point away from his duty. During ancient time, it was the duty of a righteous Brahmin to gain the knowledge of supreme soul, maintain his integrity in all walks of life, not amassing wealth and maintaining his body on alms received through begging. Sudama used to observe all the moral teachings. He used to beg at five houses daily. When some of the house owners didn't oblige him by offering anything, he never went to the sixth house to take alms.

Life isn't a uniform motion. There're waxing and waning of fortune in it. A knowledgeable person maintains his equanimity even during odd phases in life. After some time, Sudama got married. Later on his house was filled with children but he had no proper means to feed them. The local king offered him the opportunity to get appointed in his court as a court poet. He refused the proposal. A court poet had to compose poems in praise of the king. The king was very corrupt and indulged in many unethical practices. To praise such a king would be against the duty of a righteous Brahmin. To admire a corrupt person is the act of spreading corruption and giving it sanction. For refusal of king's proposal, king's men rebuked and beat him. He had accepted physical torture but didn't praise a corrupt king.

Corruption first appears in mind, and then it gets its visual appearance. Sudama did not get any chance at any place to bring prosperity to his family through lawful means and without compromising with his duty. In the beginning, his wife supported him. But she couldn't bear the suffering of her children. They were on the verge of death due to hunger. She suggested to Sudama to seek the help of his friend, Lord Krishna, who had then become the king of Dwarka. Despite his initial reluctance, to please his wife he went to meet Krishna. After a long arduous journey he reached Dwarka.

Krishna welcomed his childhood friend. Sudama was given an intimate royal treatment. After accepting his warm hospitality, he returned from Dwarka. At the moment of his departure from Dwarka, neither Sudama demanded any thing, nor did Krishna offer anything. But no one returns empty hand from the door of God.

After miles long return journey, Sudama reached his home town. He couldn't find his cottage. Instead, he saw a huge building in the place of his cottage. He thought that the local king had destroyed his cottage and had built a building on the very spot. Incidentally, his wife saw him from the window of the building. She came down and welcomed him. She told him that his friend Lord Krishna got built this huge palace and blessed us with all most all sorts of comfort and wealth. Sudama expressed his gratitude to Lord Krishna. But from the next day, he again went on his begging mission at five houses. When his wife asked that he had no need to go for such a work. He answered with the same integrity—"My duty is to seek the supreme knowledge and spread it. I can't enjoy the luxury. I've to sustain on a handful of grain offered by the five houses.

I can't relinquish my nature of self-control."

Sudama is an ideal example of integrity for all ages. Dhritrashtra had an ambition to grab the power of Hastinapura. Shakuni, the wicked uncle (*mama*), came in the court of Hastinapura and stayed there. His polluted mind had corrupting influence on Duryodhana and his brothers. This influence led to the annihilation of the entire Kuru clan.

30. Diplomacy for World Peace and Prosperity

परित्राणाय साधूनां विनाशाय च दुष्कृताम।
धर्मसंस्थापनार्थाय सम्भवामि युगे युगे॥

– गीता

paritranaya sadhunam vinashaya cha dushkritam
Dharma sansthapanaya sambhami yuge yuge

– *From* ***'Geeta'***

Meaning: *To liberate the saint and to destroy the wicked, I take birth in different ages.*

Respect and protection of each individual is equally important. Dignity of each individual is to be respected. Each culture has its own significance. Sometimes centripetal forces work vigorously and sometimes centrifugal forces trying to suppress the opposite tendencies.

The world is full of diversities. Here, no single tendency or single faith will rule over all the continents. Many dictators had dream to rule over this world but their dream shattered. Many such experiments have been failed. Alexander came to India to rule over the world. But he had to suffer ultimate loss.

Napoleon had to spend last days of his life in Saint Helena Island lonely in the prison of English men. Czar was beheaded by revolutionary forces. Hitler had to commit suicide. Saddam

Hussein was hanged by the forces of U.S.A. Osama bin Laden was killed by the soldiers of the same country. Ravana was killed by Lord Rama. Kartvirya was killed by Lord Parashurama. Kansa and thousands of demons were killed by Lord Krishna. Thus, the end of all dictators is same. They waste their life in trifles.

Some times regional aspirations rise so high that they pose threat to central rule. Sometimes central power becomes so strong that it ignores the small demand and sentiment of people at local level. Sometimes in the name of globalisation local cultures are destroyed. Sometimes in the name of industrialisation, land and property of poor peasants are captured. They're not given handsome compensation. Hence, struggle begins. Sometimes, for the sake of so called development, entire forest and locale of tribal people are annihilated. They start armed struggle to revenge their loss.

Sometimes capitalism spreads its arm to control the entire world. To counter such forces communism emerges. To resist absolute monarchs, democracy comes. To establish their control in democratic set up often corrupt forces manipulates. To protect one's economic needs protectionism becomes the law. To business in other's territories and to have a grasp in different economies, protectionism is waved.

Then multi-national culture emerges. Hence, world is integrated to a supreme economy. Any fall in the supreme economy has a global repercussion. But there are many positive influences of the confluence of economies. Many good practices are adopted. Many cultures join hands with one another.

Krishna had knowledge of all these things. He had a great respect for diversity in human life. He himself led a life full of diversity. His childhood was spent in the household of a pastoral family. People of Braja led a simple life. Their economy was based on forest product and cow. They were simpleton people.

They had no knowledge of urbane sophistication. They enjoyed a happy life but there was only one threat on their life and property. It was a threat from Kansa, the wicked king of Mathura. Krishna eliminated that threat from their life for ever.

Before Kansa, he had already eliminated many major and minor threats from their life.

When he reached Mathura, he gave happiness to the local people. But many demons continued to attack on Mathura. He couldn't get time to return Braja, a nearby area. When Jarasandha continued to harass people of Mathura, he decided to leave Mathura with his selected friends, relatives and family men. Jarasandha had personal enmity with Krishna. He had a clear understanding of this fact. Hence, he decided to leave Mathura. Some persons put others life at stake for their person enmity. Krishna had a different stuff. He was always of the opinion that peace in the society is more important than the pleasure and enmity of an individual. He decided to change his kingdom.

He shifted his kingdom to Dwarka, on the sea coast of modern Gujarat. Very soon this emerged as an important port town. Its economy flourished too. It was very difficult for Jarasandha to reach there because Jarasandha was the king of Magadha, a region in modern central Bihar. To reach Dwarka, his army had to cross many kingdoms.

Hence, it was on a strategic location. It was on the trade route between north and south India. So, this state emerged as a powerful entity. In the meantime, Dwarka tried to increase its economic and diplomatic power. Krishna made new friends in neighbouring states. His state didn't attack any neighbour state. It was in favour of peace in the Indian subcontinent. Krishna focused his attention for establishing peace in the entire subcontinent.

He suggested his friends what he believed appropriate for himself. When Pandvas were given barren land of Indraprastha, Krishna helped them to make a prosperous capital there. It was necessary to accept the infertile land. Kaurvas gave them this portion. Pandavas were mighty persons. They could wage war to get a better area as their divided kingdom but it wouldn't be a proper decision for the peace and prosperity of the entire region. In a war many innocent people are killed unnecessarily. To save life and property of the people, avoidance of war is expected. Hence, Lord Krishna helped Pandavas to build a capital on the infertile land.

Nowadays, fertile lands are used for carrying out industrial activities. Barren lands should be utilised for this purpose without disturbing the ecological balance. With the joint effort of Krishna and Pandavas the infertile territory of Indraprastha was turned into a beautiful and prosperous capital. But one hurdle remained there. Some criminal tribes were residing in the area.

They were posing threats to peace and prosperity of the region. It was very difficult for people to travel through the area. Krishna suggested Pandavas to make them friends but they didn't succumb. There was no option but to eliminate them from the area. Without making transportation peaceful, no town can achieve prosperity. Means of communication should be advanced, comfortable and hurdle free. Krishna inspired them to move in this direction. Soon, Indraprasatha become a rich state.

Yudhishthira, the eldest among Pandavas became the king of Indraprastha. He organised a royal sacrifice and invited kings from all regions. This was done by the suggestion of Lord Krishna. Many kings reached there. It was an initiative for peace.

In this sacrifice ceremony, Shishupala, an arch rival of Lord Krishna, was a guest. He tried to insult Lord Krishna. Lord had given assurance to his mother that he would forgive him for his hundred crimes but exceeding to that limit would be dangerous for him.

Then, he would be punished. Shishupal crossed that limit and Krishna cut his throat with his Sudarshana Chakra, a circular weapon used by Lord Vishnu. Krishna is said to be the incarnation of Lord Vishnu. This was the end of a wicked person's life. Another evil king, Jarasandha, was also there. He had harassed many kings and innocent people. He was a threat to the peace of entire subcontinent. He challenged the authority of Lord Krishna. It was a better occasion to end this chapter. Bhima fought a dwell with him. Krishna helped him kill

Jarasandha. Bhima followed Lord's instruction and killed Jarasandha. Lord Krishna had patience and diplomatic skill to eliminate all those who were posing threats for world peace.

He didn't allow any body's personal whims and fancy to take place in the way to peace. At the time of insulting Draupadi in the royal court of Hastinapura, Draupadi had taken a vow to wash her open hair locks with the blood of Dushasana and Bhima had taken a vow to drink the blood from Dushasana's chest and to break the thigh of Duryodhana. These two persons were in favour of war.

They were not in a compromising mood. But Lord Krishna persuaded them to send a diplomatic mission to establish peace between them. For the honour of some individuals nations shouldn't fight wars. The dignity of individuals is necessary for ensuring world peace. He himself went on a peace mission. But this mission failed. There's no harm in putting one's total effort to avoid war. When war took place, he was from the side of truth. Where there's truth, there's God, there's Lord Krishna.

31. Krishna's Contribution to Society

इहैव तैर्जितः सर्गो येषां साम्ये स्थितं मनः।
निर्दोषं हि समं ब्रह्म तस्माद् ब्रह्मणि ते स्थिताः॥

– *गीता*

Ihaiv tairjitah sargo yesham samye isthitam manah
Nirdosham hi samam brahmam tasmad brahmani te isthitah

– *From* ***'Geeta'***

Meaning: *Those who have acquired mental integrity and eaqality and are free from the bondage of life and birth , are as pure as the Supreme soul . And they dwell in Him.*

Lord Krishna is the eternal companion of mankind. He invites us to sit in the chariot beside his dear friend and favourite disciple, Arjuna. We hear the sweet sound of his flute and tumultuous sounds of drums, conchs, which are war cries. This world is full of war cries. Here most of the people fight over trifles but some others fight for genuine causes. Lord Krishna fought for all human beings. He gave a message for the welfare of entire human community. His message isn't confined to any particular sect or religion. It's transcendental. It has crossed the boundary of time and space. We imagine that under the sweet shadow of his message, we move ahead in this world. We feel that we are being taken to an entirely different world –

a world full of reassurance and inspiration. Here, peace is bestowed by profound knowledge about us and our relationship with the universe.

There're two authentic books on the life and message of Lord Krishna. We find a description of Lord Krishna's life in "Shrimad Bhagwadvata." It's a great book from devotional point of view. In the Gita, we find pure messages. In this book, the Lord says about the duties of life as well as spiritual obligations. He says that sins arise not from the nature of the work itself but from the disposition with which the work is performed. Some people perform work with an intention of getting its fruit. But some other people have detachment. When work is performed without attachment to the result, it cannot tarnish the soul or impede its quest. According to Lord Krishna, true yoga consists in the acquisition of experience and the passage through life, in harmony with the ultimate laws of equanimity, non-attachment to the fruits of action and faith in the pervasiveness of the Supreme Spirit.

He gives a great message but he respects multiplicity of faith as well. He talks about absorption of one's own self in the Supreme Soul. Here, he talks about the way of absorption. After attaining such a position, one feels a true sense of universal brotherhood. The absorption in that spirit can be attained by treading several paths. No path is to be preferred exclusively and none of them is to be disdained. The Gita emphasises upon the importance of knowledge, charity, penance and worship. It does not decry life as evil. In fact, this great book talks something above the concepts of "sacred and profane." It's a manifesto for living a better life, a blissful life irrespective of one's religious affiliations.

Lord Krishna advocated that life is sacred in itself, wherever it may be. He says that a person having true knowledge respects life in its totality. In the Gita, he says that a true scholar gives equal importance to a mean creature as well. He doesn't discriminate between a Supreme Soul and an ant. There is life in both these creatures, Lord says.

He lost his many valuable years for the welfare of mankind. He was initiated at a much later stage of life. After killing Kansa, both Krishna and Balrama were initiated by Garga Muni in the Gayatri Mantra. Later, they went to live under the care of Sandipani Muni, who instructed them in all Vedic arts and sciences in sixty-four days and nights, especially in military science, politics and spiritualism. In the beginning of this book, we have already discussed sixty-four arts which were under Krishna's command. As an offering (*guru dakshina*) to their teacher, they rescued his son from the jaws of death. Lord Krishna did not have to follow instructions from anyone else but he did follow the prevalent social norms that had been devised for the well being of mankind. He went to study at sage Sandipini's school. Hence, by doing so, Lord Krishna and his brother set a perfect example—one must accept instructions from and serve a bona fide spiritual master to advance in one's material and spiritual life. One needs guide in one's life. Without a proper guide and master and without the blessings of one's elders, one can't achieve success in one's life.

After receiving formal education, Lord Krishna stayed in Mathura for the next eighteen years. There was no need to stay there. Radha was waiting for him in Braja. Many people feeling the pangs of separation from him. But there was an impending threat of many demons on Mathura. After the death of Kansa, the rest of demons prepared to take revenge of his death. Even today, the death of a terrorist commander doesn't ensure the total end of terrorism. Other terrorists come forward to disturb peace and prosperity at the international level. Hence, Lord Krishna continued to live in Mathura. He halted the threats of many demon kings and saved Mathura. Krishna and Balrama had little time for themselves. But they had to fulfill their family obligations as well. Later, Balrama married a princess, named Revati. Lord Krishna married many women, the foremost among them being the extraordinarily beautiful queen, Rukmini. Both Krishna and Balrama established their palaces at Dwarka, a town off the coast of western India (in present-day Gujarat). They stayed at Dwarka for many years. Although Lord Krishna and Balarama were married, they exhibited the quality of detachment from material life in a perfect manner.

When Lord Krishna was about ninety years old, the great War of Kurukshetra took place. This battle brought together all the major world leaders. Lord Krishna assumed the role of a charioteer on the side of the righteous Pandavas. His elder brother, Balrama, refused to participate in the War. He went on a pilgrimage tour, blessing the entire land of India. At the start of the War, Lord Krishna displayed his stupendous Universal Form. He delivered his famous message which is known as the Bhagavad Gita, literally meaning the Song of God. This Song contains the essence of all knowledge which was spoken by the Supreme Lord Sri Krishna to Arjuna. This War concluded with the destruction of the demon kings and the reinstatement of the righteous Pandava princes as the rulers of Hastinapur. After completing their mission, Balrama and Krishna resumed their life at Dwarka; they spent some thirty-five more years at Dwarka before ending their activities on this earth.

We have the example of Lord Shiva who had drunk a deadly poison bowl to save this world at the time of mythical churning of the ocean waters. Similarly, Lord Krishna bore the brunt of many attacks on his own self. Gandhari, the mother of Duryodhana, was convinced that it was only Krishna who could have stopped the War. But, she thought, he had not done so. Due to this, she cursed him that his family shall also be destroyed. While giving the curse, her motherly emotion prevailed upon over her thinking. She forgot the injustices done to the Pandavas. She forgot the insult inflicted upon the soul of Druapadi when Dushasana had tried to remove her sari in the royal court. She had forgotten everything. Krishna accepted her curse but he didn't surrender before anything that would damage the peace and prosperity of this universe. For the betterment of the world, some people have to make sacrifice. Jesus had to sacrifice his life. Socrates had to drink hemlock. Gandhi had to sacrifice his life too. Martin Luther King had to accept death. Nelson Mandela had to spend three decades of his life in prison. Krishna had to lead a hectic life to bring harmony in the world. He delivered the message that if, under any circumstance, one had to fight a war, one must not forget one's original self. Inspiring Arjuna to fulfill his obligation and proceed on the path of action wasn't his only goal when he was delivering his Gita message. Rather, he had to give us the point—"We all are human beings. There's an immortal soul within us. The end of body doesn't mean the end of soul. The life circle is possible even beyond this life. Hence, in any case, man should do his righteous duty and contribute something positive, eternal and valuable to the evolution of human civilisation.

32. Lord Krishna's Message

यत्र योगेश्वरः कृष्णो यत्र पार्थो धनुर्धरः।
तत्र श्रीर्विजयो भूतिर्ध्रुवा नीतिर्मतिर्मम ॥

– गीता

Yatra yogeshvarah Krishno yatra Partho dhanurdharah
Tatra shrirvijayo bhootirdhruva neetirmatirmam

– *From* ***'Geeta'***

Meaning: *There's no doubt in achieving success where there are blessings of Lord Krishna , the master all sorts of yoga and the presence fighter like Arjuna , a man of action. .*

- *There's no place of confusion in life.*
- A confused person can't live a happy life.
- A confused person can't achieve success in life.
- Have faith in your own self.
- Have faith in God.
- God helps those who perform their duty with dedication.
- There's no alternative to labour.
- There must be a balance among knowledge, action and devotion.
- Every individual has a soul and this soul is

indestructible.

- For the sake of truth, one shouldn't hesitate to fight.
- Death isn't the end of life.
- Pain and pleasure are parts of life.
- One shouldn't loose his mental balance in the duality of life.
- Perform your duty without being attached to the result.
- Whatever may be the result, you concentrate on your duty.
- Try to understand yourself.
- Human life has a greater mission.
- God has given you this life. Don't waste this life over trifles.
- Lead the righteous life.
- God takes care of the man who has complete devotion.
- Work with dedication and patience; you'll win!
- If you lead righteous life, you'll have the eternal pleasure in life.
- For a welfare mission, individual's whims and fancy must be sacrificed.
- Take pure food to develop a healthy body and a sound mind.
- Before moving on a mission, you must have the clear concept of that mission.
- For getting a clear concept, understanding is must.
- Understanding comes through knowledge, experience and devotion.
- After clearing a concept, you'll have dedication.

- Respect life as whole. It is precious.
- The life of others is equally important.
- The work done with the blessings of God and due to one's own tireless dedication brings the right fruit.

There's no doubt in achieving success where there are the blessings of Lord Krishna (the master all sorts of yoga) and the presence of a fighter like Arjuna (a man of action).